Saving the Planet Without Costing the Earth

500 Simple Steps to a Greener Lifestyle

Donnachadh McCarthy

Disclaimer

The author makes all the suggestions in this book in good faith, and it is up to the individual to exercise common sense and caution in implementing his recommendations in line with their own particular circumstances. The author, publisher and their employees or agents cannot accept responsibility for loss or damage suffered by individuals as a result of following advice within this book.

First published in 2004 by Fusion Press,
a division of Satin Publications Ltd.
101 Southwark Street
London SE1 0JF
UK
info@visionpaperbacks.co.uk
www.visionpaperbacks.co.uk
Publisher: Sheena Dewan

A catalogue record for this book is available from the British Library.

ISBN: 1-904132-39-1

4 6 8 10 9 7 5

Cover and text design by ok?design

Printed on CyclusOffset,
100% recyled paper according to the RAL UZ 14 – Blue Angel
Printed and bound in the UK by Biddles Ltd, King's Lynn, Norfolk

Saving the
Planet

Without
Costing the
Earth

For Pauline, Ruth, Jenny and Becky,
my wonderful, loving, guardian angels!

Contents

Introduction

Imagine a world where ...

- Climate change did not threaten our coastlines and future food supplies.
- All our food was free from chemical contamination and genetic modification (GM).
- We had no huge landfill sites and toxic waste-incinerators.
- We were free from the diseases and cancers caused by toxic pollution.
- Our homes and industries were powered by renewable energy.
- We were self-sufficient in water supplies.
- Our extraordinarily varied wildlife was safe from extinction.

'Impossible,' I hear you murmur. Yet such a world has already existed – in fact such a world was normal for the vast majority of human existence. It was only with the Industrial Revolution that we acquired the ability to threaten the very system that enables the planet to support human activity. Indeed, there are many societies in existence today whose lifestyles are in perfect harmony with the environment in which they live. The Yanomami Indians, who incidentally started off my journey to becoming someone who cares passionately about the environment, have a lifestyle that has remained in balance with the surrounding Amazonian rainforest for millennia.

I hear you murmur again: 'This nutcase wants us to return to the Stone Age. He's mad – no one wants that!' But that is not what I'm advocating. My grandparents grew up on subsistence farms in Ireland and they lived free from chemical pollution and had a zero-waste culture. Before you mutter again, I am not about to suggest we all decamp from cities across the world to the west coast of Ireland and try and live the good life there. Rather, I am going to explain how, like nearly all personal dreams, it is possible to move towards a totally environmentally sustainable world if we really want to. And it does not necessarily mean the sacrifice of the ease and comfort of our current lifestyles. It just means that we need to be willing to learn the first steps to achieving that goal.

For instance, if you want to become a ballet dancer (which I was, before visiting the Amazon), you have to learn the five basic positions of the feet upon which ballet is based. Then week by week, with constant application, you learn gradually how to use those positions in more and more complex combinations, until eventually you are able to soar gracefully through the air like a bird. What was initially impossible has become natural!

That is how I turned my life from one that gave no thought to environmental consequences to one where I produce most of my own electricity renewably, supply a great deal of my own water and have an almost zero-waste lifestyle – step by step. I live in Peckham in inner London, so if it is possible here, it is possible wherever you live.

And that is how I would like you to use this book. It is not about guilt or painful choices. It is about learning the basic steps, so that you can gradually start to make changes in your lifestyle, and then decide how to progress towards an environmentally-friendly existence.

Chapter 1 introduces environmental auditing and gives you the tools to measure your current performance and future successes. Chapters 2 to 9 take a different issue or aspect of our lives, from how we garden to how we shop, and outline why there is a need to be environmentally sustainable in each area. Most importantly, these chapters contain lists of suggestions that you might like to take up in your own life. They are divided into four sections: ideas that will save you money, those that cost nothing to implement, those that involve a small extra expense and, finally, ideas that involve a substantial investment. *Saving the Planet Without Costing the Earth* is relevant to people of all income levels, and encourages you to do what you can within your resources. Protecting the environment is something we all are responsible for. Significantly, over 70 per cent of this book's suggestions do save you money or cost nothing – and this is one of the beauties of greener living. Chapter 1 also allows you to measure your savings from year to year.

While I have included a small number of internet addresses in these suggestions, it is best to find contacts or suppliers local to you. The easiest way is to type the issue/object into a good internet search engine (I use www.google.com) and then add your area to it. For example, if I want to find out which organic-food home delivery schemes are in my neighbourhood, I type 'organic food delivery + Peckham' into Google and press 'search'. Costs of products and services vary both within and between different countries. In order to give you an idea of the relevant costs and savings of each suggestion, I have equated the prices to everyday items such as a packet of crisps, a bottle of wine or a washing machine.

In each chapter, you will notice the implications of improving your lifestyle stretch well beyond your home. It is tempting to think that our environmental responsibilities stop at our own front door. I realised, however, that the environmental consequences of my actions at work, on holiday or in my recreational or community activities are often far, far greater than those inside my home. But that doesn't mean what I do at home pales into insignificance. On the contrary, it is what we do at home that gives us the authority to enable us to be heard when we suggest changes to our lives outside our home. Practising what we preach is one of the most powerful tools in persuading others to become more environmentally sustainable.

The final chapter is a brief account of how my life was transformed since I became environmentally aware: from being a professional dancer living in complete ignorance of the threats to our planet's ability to support life, to being a fervent environmental campaigner. It outlines some of the adventures and scrapes that I have enjoyed over the last 12 years since my encounter with the Yanomami Indians triggered this almost overnight conversion. It explains how this led to my becoming deeply involved with one of Britain's major political parties, where I have successfully campaigned for many ecological issues to be taken on board. I hope this chapter will assure you that being an environmentalist is enjoyable and can open up new doors and experiences that you may never have thought possible.

Having decided that I wanted to live a life that was as environmentally friendly as I could achieve within my then circumstances, my first steps began by scouring magazines to see what practical measures I could take. I visited green fairs and went to some wonderful education centres such as the Centre for Alternative Energy in Machynlleth, Wales. I visited Susan Roaf's groundbreaking solar-powered home in Oxford and resolved that, when I got the chance financially my own home would be as near to hers as possible in terms of sustainability (despite being an inner city 19th-century terraced cottage). This book is a distillation of that gradual personal learning curve.

Yet I have found that while my lifestyle has changed, I have not become a slave to making it environmentally friendly – a lot of it has been fun. Often it was only a small matter, such as changing from using paper tissues to linen handkerchiefs. Some changes have even made my life easier, and many of them have saved me a substantial amount of money. Returning to cycling, becoming a vegetarian and eating organic food have all had beneficial effects on my health.

Like Martin Luther King, Jr, I also have a dream. I want us humans to live in harmony with our environment. I want us to live happy, fulfilled lives that do not damage the potential of our planet to fill us with wonder or to provide for the generations following and for the vast range of wildlife that we currently share it with. If you have bought this book, then I believe that you share this dream. Use it to audit your current behaviour and decide on a list of achievable steps that you can undertake in the coming year. Then return to the book next year and see how well you have progressed and choose your new list. Thus gently, step by step, you will transform the way you live, and our dream will come closer and closer to being realised.

Chapter 1
Environmental Auditing

When you write a cheque or when you decide the budget for a holiday, you will more often than not take account of how much money you have in your bank account. You will also consider how much your monthly salary is or how much you can afford to put on your credit card and still keep up the payments without too much pain. This is a form of financial self-auditing. Companies by law have to get professional independent financial auditors to examine their books. They examine how much money was made during the previous financial year, how much of that was profitable, how much property and other assets the company owns and how much debt it has. They then produce a financial snapshot of the company at the end of their financial year in a document called the 'year-end company accounts'. The intention is to allow the shareholders, owners or the company's bankers to have good-quality and reliable information about the financial health of the company.

Environmentalists in the 1980s, searching for ways to make companies more environmentally responsible, came up with the idea of auditing a company's environmental performance. Using the term 'environmental auditing' helped business people understand the process. Environmental auditing looks at each area of activity in a company and assesses to what extent the company is fulfilling best environmental practice. Just like financial accounting, it involves measuring various inputs and outputs and assessing work practices in relation to these. A company's environmental audit will assess things such as energy, water, transport, waste production and treatment of raw materials. And just like a professional financial auditor's report, it will list the areas where problems exist and make a series of recommendations for improvement. Ideally, the environmental auditors will speak to both management and staff and the final report should be pre-submitted to the company's board and then published annually along with the company's annual report and accounts.

The nice thing about environmental auditing is that it is a gentle process. Done properly, it assesses the current situation and makes recommendations for gradual improvement within the management, human resources and financial capacity of the company. It should outline short-term, low-cost recommendations such as introducing recycling, and longer-term, capital-intensive proposals such as water recycling or improved insulation. The list of major companies that now produce annual reports on their environmental performance includes Nike, CocaCola, BT, Guinness, Black & Decker, American Airlines, The Body Shop, BP and Ford. While some may dismiss these as 'greenwash', the fact that they are even considering the subject at all is progress.

When I initially became aware of how destructive our Western lifestyles are, I resolved to reform my own into one that was more planet-benign. This was a slow learning process, but each area of my life was gradually addressed. My food, water and energy use, transport, waste, recycling etc were each dealt with steadily. It was only later that I came across the concept of environmental auditing and realised that in my own way I had already been carrying out such a process myself. This book enables you to shortcut that learning process, allowing you to implement a ready-made environmental audit of your own life.

Once I had learnt about the formal process of such auditing, I decided to take it into the wider world in which I lived.

For example, I am involved with a large voluntary national membership organisation, which has over 650 local branches across the country. Having seen the success of the environmental audit for a local housing project (see Chapter 10) and while still an ordinary member, I went along to the Annual General Meeting (AGM) of my local branch. I suggested that they should switch to using only recycled paper, and that we should send a motion to the annual national convention suggesting that the organisation should do likewise, as well as have an annual environmental audit. The other local members were supportive, and the AGM passed the motion which then went on to be successful at the national convention. As it was my first time to get anything adopted nationally, I was thrilled.

The environmental auditing process has now been in train in the organisation for nearly eight years. Our head-quarters now:

- Uses electricity supplied by a renewable energy supplier.

- Uses recycled paper for 100 per cent of its photocopying needs and nearly 100 per cent of its other publications.

- Has cut its waste production by over 50 per cent.

- Seeks the environmentally best option in all its stationery purchases.

- Has installed sensor lights in all corridors and bathrooms to eliminate wasted energy.

- Has moved from a bottled-water, drinking-fountain system to one that uses on-site filtered water.

- Buys the most energy-efficient office equipment it can find.

- Has launched a bulk recycled-paper-buying scheme for its local branches.

- Recycles all its white and coloured paper, cans and bottles.

- Has launched a nation-wide, renewable-energy affinity scheme for its own members' domestic homes.

The organisation has made a whole host of other changes to its practices arising out of the annual recommendations, and that process continues to this day. The learning process at head-office is now being used as a resource for many other sections of the organisation across Britain and even abroad. The staff understands that the organisation's integrity as one that campaigns on the environment is at risk, unless our own environmental performance is excellent. How they run their office is part of the solution.

By one person simply suggesting to a local branch to propose annual environmental auditing, the ripples are spreading out to a potentially large number of people and businesses, as the audit is now also being applied to the organisation's suppliers. But as I have said, environmental auditing is not just a useful tool for the organisations you are involved in.

Use the lists of suggestions in the following chapters and the table provided at the end of this one to carry out an environmental audit of your own home or workplace. Each idea has a box beside it to allow you to award yourself zero, one, two or three points depending on whether you never, rarely, occasionally or nearly always do something. There are five lines at the end of each chapter for you to add your own suggestions – you might well already be implementing other ingenious ideas on how to cut down your own non-sustainable energy, water or transport use, so please award yourself points for these too. There is space at the end of this chapter for you to note your Total Suggestions Score, together with readings of your gas, electricity and water meters. There are also spaces to record the amount of rubbish that you produce and the mileage on your car (or other vehicle) if you have one. When you carry out your annual audit over the coming years, you should find your environmental score growing and the energy readings steadily decreasing – and with them some of your annual financial outgoings too!

The exciting thing for me about environmental auditing is that the actual act of asking the questions puts the potential for change into our minds, which very often leads to immediate improvements. This is not an opportunity to beat yourself up because of what you are not doing. Rather it is a process where you note what you are already doing well, and the areas that need improvement. Then gradually, year by year, you put the improvements into action, according to your available time and resources. You will find that it grows steadily. Without major impositions or even noticing, you will wake up one day and find that your lifestyle has transformed itself to be substantially an environmentally responsible one.

In the lists of practical suggestions, there are ideas not only for those of you who are just starting to learn how to be more environmentally friendly, but also for those of you who are already doing a lot to care for the planet in how you live your daily lives. Make notes of the suggestions you would like to put into practice this year. Check if everything seems feasible for 12 months, given your current circumstances, and then put the notes somewhere prominent so you can easily refer back to them. For the first year, depending on how keen you are, I suggest noting between one and three things from the first three groups in each chapter and, if you can afford it, one from the whole book that requires a significant capital outlay. If this is successful, next year you could choose between two and four new items from each list, and so on. When you successfully save money by implementing some of the ideas, you should use some of it to give yourself a nice treat and use the rest to invest in your next project to improve your planet-friendly lifestyle. The key thing is to get started, and a personal environmental audit is just the tool to get you going. Every journey starts with the first step.

It is true that one person being environmentally responsible will not by itself save the planet overnight, but you will be an example to everyone you come into contact with, who will then question their own behaviour, and so the gentle revolution starts rolling!

Environmental audit

If you take your electricity, water, gas and car mileage readings, as well as your Total Suggestions Scores over five years, you will be able to see how savings come hand-in-hand with your greener lifestyle.

Total Suggestions Score

As explained earlier, in Chapters 2 to 9 you can award yourself points according to how frequently and how many suggestions you incorporate into your life. You can then record the subtotal at the end of each chapter (to allow you to consider your performance in each area) and finally the total on the table above. As you review your performance each year, you should find that your score improves by leaps and bounds!

Total Savings

Make a note of your car mileage and gas, electricity and water readings each year. In the line below each reading, you can note the cost per unit or total bill. After the first year, you can then easily calculate the amount of money saved. I have also added a line for the amount of rubbish bags you produce – although you may not pay the cost of this directly, it is still an area where a substantial change can be made and it's great to see how little waste you'll actually need to 'throw away'.

Good luck!

Date	Year 1	Year 2	Year 3	Year 4	Year 5
Total Suggestions Score					
Gas meter reading					
Cost per unit/annual bill					
Saving					
Electricity meter reading					
Cost per unit/annual bill					
Saving					
Water meter reading					
Cost per unit/annual bill					
Saving					
Car mileage reading(s)					
Cost per unit/annual bill					
Saving					
Total Savings					
Rubbish bags produced per month					

Chapter 2
Waste Not, Want Not

One of the extraordinary phenomena of our modern lifestyles is the huge waste mountain we generate. Domestic homes in the US produce over 208 million tonnes of waste every year, while German homes produce 44 million tonnes, and the UK 33 million. Our throwaway culture causes an equally vast range of environmental problems: from simple practicalities such as running out of space in which to dump the ever-increasing volumes of waste to toxic pollution leaching from these rubbish dumps and emanating from industrial incinerators. Many valuable, finite resources such as metals and plastics are being squandered so recklessly that future generations will not have the opportunity to use them. The Organization for Economic Cooperation and Development (OECD) reveals that over 10 million tonnes of metal cans are dumped each year in the world's 22 richest countries. The US gives rise to 10 million tonnes of plastic packaging waste and Italy creates 3 million tonnes of paper packaging waste every year. We are also destroying more and more of what is left of our virgin wilderness in order to feed this wasteful process. Fifty per cent of the earth's land surface has already been altered by human activities. Over 95 per cent of the USA's original forests have been felled, and 50 per cent of its wetlands drained and filled in. All of this is disastrous for thousands of species worldwide. For example, it is predicted that there will only be 10 per cent of the African great apes' habitat left undisturbed by 2030, and there will be none of the South-Asian orang-utan's territory left undisturbed. Much of this pressure is due to our wasteful lifestyle.

It is outrageous that many tribal people across the planet – who have lived in harmoniously in balance with nature for millennia – are having their precious rainsforest homes destroyed. Even more so since it is done in the search for the minerals, metals and wood that we in the West simply throw into our garbage bins after we have finished with them.

Manufacturing products from raw materials takes significant amounts of energy. For example, it takes almost a hundred times the energy to manufacture an aluminium drink can from raw ore as it does to manufacture one from an old aluminium can – yet millions of cans are thrown away each year, adding not only to the waste mountain but to climate change. And don't forget the carbon dioxide emitted by the need to transport this rubbish around the countryside.

In 2002 alone, the following were dumped in Britain:

6,000,000,000 disposable nappies

972,000,000 plastic bottles

468,000,000 batteries

42,000,000 bags of rubble

32,000,000 printer cartridges

24,000,000 car tyres

2,000,000 mobile phones

226,000 old cars

94,000 old fridges

5,600 tonnes of discarded furniture

In the US, 400 billion sheets of photocopying paper are used every year and 21 billion plastic bottles, 18 billion disposable nappies and nearly 9 million vehicles are dumped annually. And yet, just a few short decades ago, most of our grandparents and all their ancestors before them lived in an almost zero-waste culture. It is not beyond human ingenuity to recreate such a low-waste culture again, while maintaining the many comforts that our modern lifestyles give us.

I am always struck by the efficiency and beautiful simplicity of how a forest maintains its life force. Trees receive energy from the sun and combine this with the nutrients and water they draw up from the soil to create the bark, limbs and leaves that enable them to grow and flourish. The leaves drop off in autumn and fall to the ground, only to be decomposed by bacteria and insects and converted back into the nutrients that again feed the tree. The same process takes place when a branch falls off or when an entire tree dies and falls to the ground. They are converted back into nutrient-rich soil, providing the nourishment for the next generation. Given a fairly stable supply of water and sunshine, a forest can maintain itself for millennia without the need for any new outside resources. I have always felt that this philosophy should underpin our approach to our so-called rubbish. We should seek to have systems where the precious resources invested in the amazing products that facilitate our modern lifestyles should be kept within a circular recovery, recycling and re-manufacturing process. There should be no loss of materials – these are the things we value – and only a modest loss in energy (which can be replaced by renewable energies, nearly all of which in one way or another are also based on transformations of the sun's energy).

Some of this philosophy is already guiding some people in industry. A wonderful example of this in practice is the Aylesford paper recycling plant. Some people still think that recycled paper is more polluting than paper produced from felled trees: the old approach for both recycled and tree-pulp paper was to use massive amounts of water with seriously-polluting bleaching agents to pulp and clean the raw materials to produce nice white papers. However, Aylesford has incorporated revolutionary new processes.

Instead of dumping hundreds of thousands of litres of polluted water at the end of the paper-manufacturing process, they capture the water, separate out the bleaching agents, and use them to start the process all over again with the next batch of waste paper. What a simple, beautiful engineering concept! If all industrial plants could adopt this approach, many of our current waste problems could be substantially eliminated. Every home and commercial outlet has various waste products and different approaches will need to be adopted depending on individual circumstances. However, there are a few simple rules that have almost become international clichés but are absolutely valid. They can be summed up by the phrase 'reduce, reuse and recycle'. The most important rule is to try to reduce the amount of waste you produce in the first place. Then you should try to reuse any waste you still produce, and any waste then left over you should try to recycle. In my own home, I have found that waste reduction is really about a whole series of individual small decisions. They range from buying toothbrushes with replaceable heads, in order to avoid the unnecessary disposal of the plastic handle every time the head wears out, to buying my potatoes in bulk, to avoid a whole series of unnecessary small plastic bags. It requires thinking about every product that we buy to see if there are ways of reducing the amount we dump in our waste bins.

I recycle all my glass bottles and cans in the council recycling bins. When I began, there was no paper collection scheme, so I contacted a paper manufacturer who was offering a recycling scheme, which raised money for local charities. In return for my keeping an eye on their recycling bin, they paid a fee to a charity of my choice, based on the weight of paper collected. I contacted the council and got their permission to place the bin in the car park opposite my home. It was great to see how many of my neighbours took to using it almost overnight. Over the six years of operation, we raised nearly £500 for our local environmental charity to plant trees in the local park.

However, as important as recycling the waste you cannot reuse is, it is also important to try and help create a market for recycled products or they will just sit unwanted and unused. Keep an eye out when shopping in your local supermarket or on the net for alternative products made from recycled materials.

As I describe later in Chapter 5, I got a friend of mine to build me a composting structure at the end of the garden from bricks we rescued from local skips. Nearly a third of the weight of our rubbish is compostible (ie organic material which rots) and paper products make up on average another third. By removing just these two items alone, the amount of rubbish in my waste bin was immediately reduced by two thirds. Adding to this many of the waste-reduction tips included in the list below, I have managed to reduce the amount of rubbish my home produces from an average of one large black refuse bag a week to just one plastic carrier bag a month.

To work out how much rubbish you are producing a month, empty all the bins around your house on the first day of a month and then count how many bin bags you fill by the month's end. I am astonished when I walk down my street at how some households manage to produce grossly overflowing bins every week! Having successfully sorted out most of my waste, I am pleased I don't need to have a rubbish bin outside my front door, although this was the result of a comical scene with my local council's bin-men. The council had decided to introduce a new wheelie-bin (large plastic square rubbish bin on wheels) service and I happened to be in when they came to deliver the new bins to every home on my street. I came out and politely said I didn't need one. However the bin-men said that I had to have it and proceeded to wheel it onto my front path. I gently pushed it out again and said no I did not, as I recycled my waste and had no need of one. Such a concept did not compute! He then again pushed it in and I pushed it out and this went on pantomime style until he eventually gave in and moved onto the next home! It really was quite funny.

That was approximately seven years ago and the council has not had to empty any bins from my home ever since, saving them not only collection costs but also disposal costs. Instead, just once a month I drop my small plastic bag of waste into the nearest public rubbish bin.

However, while my own personal waste mountain has become more of a molehill, the UK's waste mountain has continued to grow at an alarming three per cent every year, despite all the nice words mouthed about recycling. The UK now produces a whopping 180 *million* tonnes of rubbish every year and, to our shame, at 11 per cent, we have one of the lowest recycling rates in Europe. Germany, Austria, Switzerland and the Netherlands all recycle more than 50 per cent of their household waste. In the US, over 30 per cent of such waste is either recycled or composted. Nevertheless, in some parts of the US landfill capacity is now down to less than five years, and Japan has only three years of industrial and ten years' municipal landfill capacity to go. Most UK landfill sites are predicted to be full by 2010. Unsurprisingly, in view of the not exactly pleasant odours and leakage of toxic pollution from such sites into the surrounding areas, it is becoming almost impossible to get planning permission to develop new landfill sites. Nobody wants one on their backdoor. The UK Government's response is a proposed expansion of the current network of 15 incinerators to over 115 – an almost tenfold increase.

If ever you want to get a feel for how all our individual waste streams add up into a huge environmental problem, try to visit a large waste incineration plant. I was invited to visit an enormous facility near my home, a few years ago. But what daunted me was not the size of the incinerator itself but the queue of full, extra-large articulated trucks waiting to empty their contents into the plant's insatiable stomach. They were arriving at a rate of almost one every three minutes. The massive amount of rubbish we simply dump is shocking.

But there is no use in just blaming governments, incineration companies or the local authorities if we haven't started putting our own homes in order! The amount of rubbish that you personally put in your bin is the start of the rubbish chain. There is a whole range of ideas below to help you begin. If you start taking action today, you will be amazed at how quickly and easy it is to make your overflowing garbage bins a thing of the past.

How to score

3	if you do the suggestion nearly all the time
2	if you do it occasionally or fairly often
1	if you hardly ever do it
0	if you never do it

Suggestions that save money

1   Instead of sending traditional greeting cards, use electronic ones. There are loads of such greeting companies on the web that you can select from.

Over 8 billion greetings cards are sold each year in the US, which involves the felling of over 2 million trees. And of course, nearly all of these end up in the waste bin. Sending an e-card will also save you the cost of a card, envelope and stamp!

2   You should be able to avoid the need to buy new black bin bags at home by reusing plastic shopping or packaging bags for your rubbish instead, but if you do have to buy some, make sure they're made from recycled plastic.

By eliminating your use of black plastic rubbish bags, you can save yourself a modest amount of money each year as well as reducing the use of petrochemicals used in plastic bag manufacture. Every tonne of plastic bags reused or recycled saves 11 barrels of oil. Recycled plastic bags are actually cheaper in my local supermarket than non-recycled plastic bags.

3   Next time you buy a camera, make sure it's digital.

As well as avoiding the toxic chemicals involved in film processing, which can include silver halide, hydroquinone, aminophenols, muriatic acid and ammonium thiosulfate, you also save the cost of more than two glasses of wine for each film you used to purchase and develop.

4   Avoid as far as possible the use of disposable razors. Buy a traditional one that uses replacement blades.

A mainstream brand of blade costs a little less than a disposable razor.

5   Try using a shaving brush instead of those appalling foam spray cans. It literally takes 30 seconds to brush up a lather with a piece of soap. The shave is every bit as good, despite all the millions they spend on advertising to tell you the opposite!

A shaving brush can be bought for a little bit more than a typical can of shaving foam but can last a lifetime. The time taken to create the lather with a brush is no longer than the time it takes to shake a tin of shaving foam. I have found that there is no need for the so-called shaving soap, as ordinary soap lathers up perfectly well.

6   Find a supplier for toothbrushes with replaceable heads. It makes no sense to throw away millions of perfectly good toothbrush handles merely because the head is worn.

While a toothbrush designed for replaceable heads costs a little more than an ordinary toothbrush, the heads cost less than half the price of a disposable toothbrush. That can work out at saving the price of a new shirt annually if you are a four-member family and you eliminate 16 wasted plastic toothbrush handles from your waste stream to boot.

7   Use cotton nappies (diapers) instead of disposable ones. There is a new generation of cloth nappies that are made to fit babies snuggly and use velcro instead of pins. Disposable nappy liners can be flushed down the toilet for the unpleasant messy bits. Wash the nappies yourself or use a local washing service if there is one.

Three billion nappies are disposed of a year in the UK: that's over four per cent of our total waste. Fourteen billion disposable nappies are dumped every year in the US. Organic cotton nappies each cost about ten times that of a disposable nappy but can be used over and over, whereas the disposable nappies can be used only once and remain almost forever in a landfill. It is estimated that you can save approximately the price of a new washing machine for each child by switching from disposable to reusable nappies.

8   Use a reusable sanitary product such as the rubber Mooncup. This is worn internally and forms a seal with the lining of the vaginal wall and can hold up to a third of the monthly flow, which can then be emptied, washed and

replaced until your period ends. You simply empty it the same number of times that you usually replace your tampons or sanitary pads.

These cost about the equivalent of three bottles of wine and last up to ten years. The company supplying them offers a full refund if you are not happy with the product. As well as avoiding putting potentially toxic materials into your body, there is obviously a potential cost saving within a year. It also saves perpetuating a market for heavily pesticide-raised cotton and avoids all the related packaging and waste.

9   Carefully open the plastic wrappers that magazines and other products come in and use them as freezer or sandwich bags.

Presuming you use them for work sandwiches, you might save five small bags per week. This works out at a potential saving that could buy you four bottles of organic wine per year!

10   Reuse envelopes by simply peeling the address labels off envelopes that you receive through the post.

White A4 (letter-sized) envelopes cost as much as a regular postage stamp each, whereas the regular triple folded letter size (DL) cost about a third of that.

11   Cut scrap paper into suitable size for a notepad and stick them together with a staple or find a little box to hold them in a convenient place, eg beside the phone.

You really should never need to buy notepaper for notes around the house.

12   Instead of throwing away old clothes, create a brand-new wardrobe by simply dying them.

A packet of washing-machine dye costs about the same as a pair of good socks. You simply place the dye in the machine with a packet of salt, run a washing cycle, and you have a new wardrobe without spending the money on new clothes. I discovered I wasn't using a whole range of my clothes because they had a stain or were a bit faded, even though the cloth was perfectly good. By dying them I had suddenly gained a new range of clothes that would have cost the equivalent of more than half a new washing machine. Dying can also cut down on your cotton use. Non-organically grown cotton accounts for over a quarter of worldwide pesticide use, with each pair of jeans using the equivalent of 333g (11.7 oz) of pesticide. Its production in Uzbekistan has been largely responsible for the Aral Sea becoming too polluted with pesticides to support fish. Millions of migratory bird deaths in the US are attributed to the heavy use of pesticides in the cotton industry.

13   Borrow books from a local library rather than buying new ones.

As most libraries allow free borrowing, this will significantly reduce your reading costs. They also often have a low-cost, book ordering service, where you can request that they buy a book that you wish to read.

14   Do a regular clear out of your bookshelves and music collections, selling unwanted books, DVDs, CDs, videos and records etc to the second-hand shop or donate them to your local charity shop.

Allowing your collections to be reused rather than sitting unused on your shelves can not only make you some money with which to buy new items, but allows other people to buy second-hand products, reducing the raw material used for new ones. CDs for example use the following materials in their manufacture and packaging: polycarbonates, phthalocyanine, silver, polypropylene and cardboard.

15   Rather than buying them, hire DVDs, videos and CDs from a rental shop or check out your local library to see if they lend them.

My local DVD-rental prices are easily one sixth of the purchase price. Some local libraries rent them out for long periods at even lower costs.

16   If you have time, visit the reference section of your local library to read the daily newspaper instead of buying one.

This will help reduce raw material production (trees!) and the huge waste paper mountains that follow.

17   If you do need to buy new products for your home, see if there are good-quality ones available second-hand first. Check the classified section of your local paper or local notice boards in libraries and outside shopping cen-tres, as well as websites such as eBay.com.

As well as finding a cheaper product, you are helping to reduce the amount of products that are dumped unnecessarily because of a lack of a second-hand market.

18   If you want to buy new books, CDs, DVDs and videos try your local second-hand stores or local charity shops first to see if they have what you are looking for. Better still, you could download your music choices via the web and store them on your computer.

Reuse of such objects reduces our waste mountain and can make you or a local charity some money.

19   Use cotton or linen handkerchiefs rather than paper tissues.

A cloth handkerchief costs less than a box of paper tissues but will last for years, while paper tissues last for only a couple of sneezes.

20   If you end up with unused paper napkins when eat- □
ing out or receive tissue wrapping around bought goods,
save them and place them in a little box near the toilet and
use them instead of toilet paper.

*More often than not, napkins will be simply thrown in the bin
by the takeaway or restaurant where you have eaten. Millions
of unused and clean paper napkins get thrown away like this
every year. A friend of mine did this and found he hardly
needed to buy any more toilet paper for personal use. Of
course if you live in the countryside and want to be even
greener, you might consider using dock leaves, which have a
wonderful soothing quality on your bum! This can eliminate all
the processing, packaging, dying, transport and cost required
for your toilet paper!*

21   Compost all kitchen waste.   □

*Using compost instead of bought fertilisers saves you money,
the pollution involved in a trip to the garden centre and the
unnecessary transport involved in removing your waste from
your home by garbage trucks. Even if you don't have access to
your own garden, a tiger-worm compost bin will fit in your
kitchen and the soil they magically produce can be donated to
a suitable local, green open space.*

22   Compost all your garden waste.   □

*Like kitchen waste, nearly all garden waste is composed of over
95-per-cent water. Therefore, using precious energy resources
to transport it to faraway landfill sites does not make sense.
Composting it in your own garden eliminates this waste.*

23   If you use a pen a lot at home or at work, consider □
buying a fountain pen.

*This will last you a lifetime. Even the inkbottle used for refilling
the fountain pen is recyclable.*

24   Shop at bring-your-own container stores.

Some shops specialise in allowing you to bring your own containers to fill up with loose dry products such as rice and muesli, which are often cheaper than packaged goods. See if there is one in your neighbourhood – they eliminate packaging completely.

25   Also see if you can buy black tea or herbal teas loosely and buy a tea-dunker.

This removes the need for the tea bags, boxes, plastic and foil wrapping, thread, staples that are otherwise needed for a simple cup of herbal tea!

26   Better still, grow your own tea-making herbs, such as peppermint and lemon verbena. You can have your own delicious herb tea by simply plucking the leaves and putting them in boiling water. It really impresses your guests.

You can grow peppermint from seed or plants that can be bought very cheaply at your local garden centre. Be warned – a bunch of fresh mint from the supermarket will cost you almost as much as a new plant, usually comes heavily wrapped in plastic and of course will not give you years of fresh leaves.

27   See if there are any local shops that supply goods such as potatoes in bulk, to avoid wasteful packaging.

Bulk buying will save you money as well as eliminating waste plastic packaging. Large bags of potatoes are often in brown paper bags which can be thrown on the compost heap, thus eliminating all waste.

28   Save leftover scraps of candle wax, buy some candlewick and then make your own candles.

Saves you buying new candles and eliminates transport and packaging environmental costs.

29   Think seriously whether you really need to have a new pet.

While they do give pleasure, do bear in mind that having a pet can be harmful to the local environment.

Birds were really meant to fly and not be stuck in cages.

Fish were meant to be in ponds, lakes, rivers and seas and not in little glass tanks.

Dogs are pack animals and do not naturally sleep on couches all day, waiting for their human pack to come home after work!

Worldwide there are over 400 million domestic cats, with over 8 million in the UK and 60 million in the US. That means approximately 2,816,000,000 empty tins of cat food every year in the UK, and then there's the used cat litter. Over a fifth of the world's tuna catch goes into US cat food alone. Hundreds of millions of birds are killed every year by cats, with estimates of over a billion small mammals also being killed every year in the States. It is estimated that 55 million birds are killed by cats each year in the UK. Among the most commonly killed are house sparrows and starlings, whose populations are in decline across Britain. Cats are even more of a threat when they live near precious wildlife sites as they often can kill rare or endangered species.

30   Consider choosing to have no more than two of your own children.

The planet already has 6 billion people packed on to it. We are fast consuming all the remaining space for the other animals that live on our planet as well as damaging the earth's ability to sustain its biosphere for future generations.

31   You can now even choose to provide for sustainable ways of disposing of your remains after you die. The wood, lining and metals used for traditional coffins,

the formaldehyde used in embalming, the energy used by crematoria and the pollution emitted by them – all have environmental costs attached. Rather than wasting land in those awful marble-bestrewn ecological waste-lands people call graveyards, sign up for a green grave-yard. There are a number of options including ones where your grave will make up future woodland, and others run by wildlife charities. The purchase price of the grave goes towards the purchase of the land and a fund for its perpetual maintenance, and trees are then plant-ed on the graves.

There are now over 170 green graveyards in the UK alone. Some German states have now legalised woodland burial sites and the first green burial ground in Italy has been founded in Milan. While the green burial movement has yet to take off in the US, Canada or Australia, there are a handful already operating. The Natural Death Centre's website contains an international list of green-burial sites in English speaking coun-tries, so you can check to see if there is one near you at www.naturaldeath.org.uk. Prices vary but nearly all are sig-nificantly cheaper than traditional burials or cremations, with savings of well over 50 per cent common. (In England an aver-age plot costs about the same price as a new washing machine.)

32   Let people know in your will that you are to be buried in a cardboard coffin rather than in a wasteful timber coffin.

There are also environmentally friendly coffins available made from woven willow. You can even get recycled cardboard coffins through the post! (These cost from as little as the cost of two pairs of new jeans.)

Suggestions that cost nothing

33   Avoid unnecessary packaging when shopping. A whole chapter could be written on this one! It means that if there is a choice between unwrapped avocados and avocados in a plastic wrapped carton, for goodness sake buy the unwrapped avocados! And there is no need to put them in a plastic bag just to take them to the checkout. Choose the cereal that is packed simply in a plastic bag to one that is in a plastic bag inside an unnecessary cardboard box. Choose the T-shirt that is available to buy loose over the one in the plastic and cardboard packaging. Choose the sausages in the plastic wrapping over that in the cardboard-surrounded plastic-box packaging or choose those in a cardboard box with no plastic wrapping.

By doing the above, you will not only reduce the amount of waste leaving your home, you will help avoid the waste in resources involved in manufacturing unnecessary packaging in the first place (and the pollution involved in their manufacture). Your spending power also communicates itself to the manufacturers, who will see that there is a market for 'less wrapped' products.

34   Always have a spare plastic bag on you when you go out in case you suddenly need one if shopping.

It is estimated that nearly 750 billion plastic bags are used worldwide every year. The US alone uses over 12 million barrels of oil to make its plastic bags every year; the vast majority of which end up in landfill sites. In Taiwan, it is estimated that every resident uses over 900 plastic bags every year.

35   Buy yoghurts and other food products where available in biodegradable cellulose containers rather than plastic ones.

Biodegradable cellulose is renewable because it is made with fibres from natural sources such as wood or cotton. Plastic containers use up precious non-renewable oil resources and their manufacture involves the use of carcinogenic chemicals and high levels of energy due to high temperatures required for the manufacture of synthetic plastics.

36   Bring small, clean, reused bags if going to the supermarket for vegetables and fruit. These can be got via re-using previously purchased small plastic bags or from the plastic wrappers that magazines or other products that you buy come in.
This will reduce the number of unwanted, used, small plastic bags in your waste bin.

37   Do not flush your used sanitary pad but rather bag it in a reused bag or its plastic packaging and bin it instead.
Seventy-five per cent of blocked drains are caused by flushing sanitary protection. Binning it also saves the plastic components from littering beaches. Also see point number 8 in this chapter for an alternative to disposable sanitary products.

38   Use hedge clippings as mulch rather than throwing them in the bin. Just simply throw them on your borders.
They keep weeds down while decomposing and enriching your soil naturally. Throwing your own gardens nutrients into your garbage bin simply does not make sense.

39   If you use wooden pencils, throw the parings into the compost bin.
As they are wood; they will decompose naturally.

40   Recycle all your tin cans, plastic bottles, old clothes, glass, paper, card etc.
This can reduce your waste stream by up to nearly two-thirds.

41   If you are getting rid of any old tools, see if there is

a charity operating in your area like the Work Aid Charity, which sends refurbished tools to people in need in developing countries, or give them to a charity shop.

It eliminates them from your waste stream and can make money for the charity.

42   Ensure that you dispose of old batteries responsibly with your local council (if you really have to use them!)

While quite toxic if they leak into the environment, battery components can be very easily recycled.

43   If you buy honey and jam from a local supplier you can return the jars to them at the end of the year for reuse.

It will not save you money but is a fun way of keeping jars circulating usefully in your local community, eliminating the need for the supplier to buy new jars.

44   Use reusable glass milk bottles rather than cartons where available. I found that my local shops have phased out ordinary milk bottles, but still used them for sterilised milk. I tried this out even though I was used to pasteurised milk and found it fine, so switched over in the interests of avoiding a small mountain of plastic milk bottles in my waste bin.

Plastic and cardboard milk containers can make up a significant amount of waste in your bin, especially if your local authority does not recycle plastic. Glass milk bottles are reused up to an average of 18 times.

45   For personal toiletries such as hand cream or shampoo try to buy from retailers that offer refillable containers or recycling facilities such as The Body Shop. Avoid the use of individual sachets of shampoo or shower gel as much as possible.

This will reduce the waste stream from your bathroom waste bin.

46   Consider your use of personal toiletries such as shampoo and consider whether you can reduce the amount you are using.

Most hair types do not need shampooing every day, even in the city.

47   Sign up with a service that removes you from junk mail databases.

I was delighted at the massive drop in junk mail that came in my front door within weeks of my signing up for such a service. It really does work. In the UK you simply register online at www.fpsonline.org.uk and in the US at www.dmcconsumers.org. For other countries check the web to see if there is a relevant service. Many countries, such as Germany and Belgium, do also have such systems. If there isn't one, ask Friends of the Earth or another environmental campaigning organisation to campaign for one! While you still receive junk mail, make sure you recycle.

48   Sign up with a fax preference service.

This removes you from junk fax lists, which at a stroke eliminates almost all unsolicited faxes, reducing the amount of fax paper and ink used, and also the amount of time spent reading marketing materials you aren't interested in. In the UK, you can register at the same website as the mail preference service www.fpsonline.org.uk. It takes 28 days for both services to take effect.

49   For junk mail that gets past the mail preference service, simply write on the envelope 'return to sender – please remove me from your database'. Pop it in the postbox or alternatively, if you have opened it, write on the letter that you wish to be taken off their mailing list and put it into the reply-paid envelope and send it off.

This saves the frustration of receiving your tenth prize winning draw from Readers Digest, hundredth opportunity to sign up for an American Express Card or your thousandth free AOL CD – think of the freedom!

50   Make 'a no junk mail please' sign for your letterbox.   ☐
This can stop your plague of unwanted home-delivery pizza leaflets.

51   If eating an apple or banana outdoors, seek a hedge   ☐
to discreetly deposit the core/skin in to naturally decompose, rather than dumping it in a garbage bin.
Reduces amount of biodegradable waste unnecessarily transported.

52   Before buying something, always ask yourself if this   ☐
is something that you really want. Think if you would rather spend the money on an experience instead, such as an acupuncture session or a sauna.
Buying an experience rather than a product eliminates the need for the raw materials used in its production and packaging.

53   Rather than simply buying even more consumer   ☐
products for someone's birthday or Christmas present, buy them an experience instead that uses no resources, eg a holistic massage or a trip to the theatre, a dance performance or the cinema. Alternatively you could buy them an organically grown fruit tree (if they have a garden) or fruit shrub (if they have a balcony or window box).
An organically grown apple tree can be bought for the cost of three bottles of ordinary wine. Organically reared blackcurrant or gooseberry bushes can be got for less than two bottles. A non-organic strawberry bush can be got for the cost of a half litre of beer.

54   Old mobile phones can usually be recycled. Again,   ☐
check on the web for local schemes. Over 100 million

mobile phones are thrown away each year in the US and over 2 million in the UK.

Recycling these removes a complex product from the waste stream, which can contain nickel, cadmium, ferrous metals, various plastics and small amounts of gold, copper, palladium and platinum. As well as saving the environment, you can often make money for local charities.

55   Phone directories can be recycled by a number of routes. Check with your local authority's recycling information line or the telephone company's website for information about where your nearest scheme is.

Millions of phone books are wastefully dumped each year. Make sure you do not add to the phone book mountain!

56   If you are in a situation where you are unable to have children of your own or you want a larger family than two, consider adopting.

Does it really make sense to go to the trouble and medical expense of having your own children when there are literally millions of orphans without anyone to care for them on this planet already?

Suggestions that cost a small amount extra

57   If buying tampons, try and buy the new ranges of tampons made from 100-per-cent-organic cotton, many of which avoid the use of chlorine bleach.

Organic tampons can currently cost nearly twice as much as regular ones, but as well as helping to tackle the awful pollution involved in cotton growing, you are also avoiding putting pesticide-grown materials into your body.

58   Buy a strong, reusable shopping bag rather than using plastic shopping bags.

While involving a small initial financial cost, it eliminates that mountain of used plastic bags that accumulates in the back of our cupboards.

59 When buying brand-new products, buy as good quality as you can afford.

☐

When I buy cheap socks, they only last about three months, whereas some good-quality ones I bought are still going strong 12 years later! This not only reduces waste but it is better value for money in the long run.

Suggestions that require a significant capital investment

None.

Other suggestions

1 _____ ☐

2 _____ ☐

3 _____ ☐

4 _____ ☐

5 _____ ☐

_____

	Year 1	Year 2	Year 3	Year 4	Year 5
Suggestions Score (subtotal)					

Chapter 3
The Water of Life

Water is a precious commodity. It makes up almost two-thirds of the human body. Our planet is covered in huge oceans, but less than two per cent of the earth's water is salt-free fresh water, and that includes the amount stored (admittedly fast disappearing) in glaciers and subterranean aquifers. The fresh water actually available to us for human consumption, maintaining our food supply and keeping nature green, is a tiny percentage of the total global water supply – estimates put the amount as low as 0.02 per cent. It is feared that some of the wars of the 21st century will be fought over water supplies.

A recent UN report found that global water use has increased sixfold over the last century, at twice the rate of population growth. About 40 per cent of the world population – more than 2 billion people – face water shortages, and by 2025 that figure is expected to increase to 50 per cent.

Agriculture represents 70 per cent of this consumption. The greatest drain on the world's freshwater supplies in agricultural and developing countries is inefficient irrigation systems. In the West, due to the fact that many of our heavy industries have been transferred to the developing world (which of course just exports the problem), our industrial use of water has levelled out – but our domestic use of water is soaring. Global environmental disasters such as the poisoning of the Aral Sea and the expansion of the Sahara Desert are caused by destructive human activities. These not only damage our human economic well-being, but destroy the habitats and populations of our fellow creatures. However, some new industrial plants are increasingly installing water-efficiency measures to reduce the cost of this raw material. Which is a good example of a positive side of market forces kicking in. Some of the new industrial processes are really quite revolutionary in how they recycle water, and so are exciting from an environmental point of view.

I first became interested in water as an environmental issue during the dry, hot summers of the early 1990s. Newspaper stories described the environmental consequences of draining rivers around London to supply its water needs. Photographs of formerly beautiful rivers, drained to flush our toilets and water our gardens, destroyed my complacent and wasteful Western approach to water use in my home.

Draining rivers reduces oxygen levels for fish and other water creatures. The reduced flow means that pollution from 'legitimate' sources such as industry and sewage plants becomes more concentrated, leading to further dangers for wildlife. Many creatures depend on a plentiful water supply for breeding and on wet riverbanks for their food. Low river levels also mean that less fresh water flows into river estuaries. The resulting higher levels of salination cause difficulties for the fish and other wildlife that have adapted over hundreds of years to the mixed waters of the estuaries. Threatened species include the otter, great crested newt, Atlantic salmon and creeping marshwort. Many precious wildlife habitats – rich marshlands, fens, swamps and wet grasslands – are all threatened due to human activities and climate change, both in industrial and developing countries around the globe. Many habitats face the opposite threat; that of being flooded with salt water due to rising sea levels.

Less than one per cent of the water piped to our homes (all of which is drinkable) is actually used as drinking water, and demand for water in our homes is predicted to increase by another 40 per cent over the next 30 years. We already use over four times more water than our great-grandparents at the beginning of the 20th century. The amount has tripled in the last 30 years alone. The UK is one of the worst offenders, using almost four times more water per person than Belgium and 15 times more than the average developing country. The average North American uses 796,000 cm^3 of water per annum, while the average inhabitant in Oceania uses only 47,000 cm^3.

Water-supply companies invest billions to ensure security of supply for our ever-increasingly voracious appetites for clean water. Annual capital investment by the water industry is currently running at over £3 billion pounds a year in Britain and yearly running costs are over £2.5 billion. In the US, over $1 trillion dollars in investment is thought to be needed to maintain water quality and supplies over the next 20 years. This investment has not only environmental consequences, because it means collecting and draining more water from rivers, lakes and aquifers, but also of course means bigger bills for the customer.

Just think about the following: the average house in England has on average 35,000 litres (9,100 US gallons) of water falling on its roof each year, while the average in Germany has 42,000 litres (10,920 US gallons) and New York has 56,000 litres (14,560 US gallons). Most of us pay, by some method, to have all that rainwater pumped away (in the UK, this is included in the sewage section of your water rates). That rainwater is then purified, using processes that often include chemicals such as chlorine and aluminium sulphate. It is then pumped back to our homes, where over a third of this drinking quality water is promptly flushed down our toilets or used for watering plants and gardens. This journey from rooftop to toilet can involve kilometres worth of travel for the water. No engineer in their right mind would design such a horrendously inefficient system from scratch, yet this is what we have ended up with. Yet, with a rain-harvester installed in your home, this journey can be reduced to just a few metres!

Many people are unaware of the energy it takes to transport water. I was gob smacked to find that the transportation of water uses up to four per cent of the UK's entire energy use. This energy is used simply to move around, often unnecessarily, a substance that falls on our own roofs. Up to five nuclear-power stations could be shut down tomorrow if we could avoid the necessity of transporting this water. And of course we consumers are paying for the cost of this energy.

This knowledge really fired up my determination to sort out my water use. I didn't want to contribute to climate change or to bequest nuclear waste to succeeding generations. I also didn't want to play a role in the drying out of local rivers. The idea of otters scurrying around desperately on dry river edges, or of fish gasping for oxygen as a result of my water wastage did not sit well on my conscience.

So I sought out a friendly plumber who installed a rain-harvester on the roof of my downstairs toilet. We designed it so that the rainwater falling on the main roof of the house is diverted from the roof-gutters into a small filter tank, and from there is stored in a medium sized tank on the roof of the toilet. A pipe leading from this automatically fills the toilet cistern using gravity. I have found that this small-scale system has provided me with over 80 per cent of my toilet's water needs. For most of the remaining 20 per cent, I use water saved from the shower (I stand in a large plastic basin while under it), so I am almost totally independent of the mains system for my toiletwater. There is also a tap in the bathroom on the down pipe from the rain-harvester (on it's way to the toilet), from which I take small amounts of water for my household plants, soaking my kitchen dishes and for other non-potable uses around the house.

Washing (and dishwashing) machines can vary greatly in their water usage. So when I needed a new washing machine, I bought myself the most water-economical model on the market. It was energy and detergent efficient too. I also installed a rain barrel to collect the rain from the kitchen roof, which was not connected to the toilet's rain-harvester system.

I now avoid watering my lawn in summer, deciding that it is natural for grass to turn brown in droughts and, more often than not, it recovers within hours of receiving the gift of a summer shower. I use the rain barrel to water my potted plants, tomatoes and herbs and to ensure that my favourite shrubs or fruit bushes survive any summer drought in a healthy state. I place hedge clippings on top of the soil in my borders as I discovered that mulching (the spreading of organic materials on top of the soil) helps reduce water loss in summer. I also use kitchen dishwater and the waste water from my washing machine to help extend the lifetime of the supply in the rain barrel by throwing it on the garden. The result of these efforts is that I have had to resort to tap water on only a very few occasions over the last ten years to keep my garden alive. One of the pleasant but unexpected side effects of having a rain-harvester in my home has been to change my relationship with rainy days for the better. Now when it rains I often perk up and think, 'Oh good! My rain-harvester is filling up again!'

Having made a good start sorting out my home's water use, I found myself taking this message out to other areas of my life. I successfully persuaded my local council to require property-developers to install rainwater barrels when they were building new homes in the area. I was so chuffed when I peeked over the fence of a new, local housing estate across the road from me and saw a shiny row of bright new green rain-barrels in their back gardens. This meant that these households won't have to go to the expense of retrofitting rain barrels and can use rainwater to reduce their water bills, as these houses have been fitted with water meters.

We also persuaded our local authority to introduce a monitoring programme for its own water use. We used the example of another council (Kirklees) in the north of England, who introduced a water-efficiency programme and saved over 127 million litres (33 million gallons in the US) of water a year from their council premises. This shaves £300,000 off their annual water bill, which can be used for other of the council's more essential services, such as for children or the elderly. Being able to quote this to our local councillors greatly helped mobilise their support.

With the increasing introduction of water metering in the home, a new culture of respect in individuals for the economic as well as the environmental cost of water is emerging. According to the OECD, over two thirds of the world's richest 25 countries already meter the water supply to over 90 per cent of their houses. Germany and France are increasingly metering apartments. While this is good, governments and local authorities must ensure that social housing for poorer people has all the most up-to-date, water-efficiency measures installed, or have any extra water costs taken into account with benefits or tax credits, so that the poor don't suffer as a result of the introduction of water metering.

The way you use water in your home is a crucial part of contributing to a better environment. Don't forget that if the water you are wasting is hot water, eg by running the hot tap while shaving, you get a double whammy as you are wasting not only the energy used to clean and pump the water to and from your home, but also the energy used to heat it. You can use the suggestions below as a means to assess your own water usage and gain ideas about how you can start taking steps to address your own home's water usage. Indicated financial savings are for homes that are water metered. If you pay a flat fee charge, you will not make any direct financial savings, but of course the environmental savings are still absolutely relevant.

As they say in Gaelic 'Slainte an bradan leat'! (May the health of the salmon be with you!)

How to score

3	if you do the suggestion nearly all the time
2	if you do it occasionally or fairly often
1	if you hardly ever do it
0	if you never do it

Suggestions that save you money

60   Put a plug in the basin when you are washing.

Washing your face or whatever with the tap running is extremely wasteful of precious clean drinking water. If you run it for five minutes, you can waste more than 50 litres (13 US gallons), when with a plug, half a sinkful would only use about 8 litres (2.1 US gallons) and do exactly the same job.

61   Have a shower rather than a bath.

With an average three-minute shower using 30 litres (7.8 US gallons) and a bath anything between 80 and 200 litres (between 20.8 and 52 US gallons), this means that for a household of four people, the annual difference could be as much as 240,000 litres (62,400 US gallons) annually.

62   Avoid the installation of power-showers.

These use up to twice the amount of water that a normal shower uses or four times what an aerating shower head uses, with the added cost of energy used for heating the water, and you end up no cleaner!

63   Do not run the tap while brushing your teeth.

If you spend a minute brushing your teeth, and you turn the tap on to wet your toothbrush before applying the toothpaste and leave it on until you are finished and have rinsed your toothbrush, you will use up to eight litres of water! Alternatively, if you turn off the tap when you are not using the water, you can wash your teeth perfectly hygienically with 0.02 litres (0.005 gallons). This saves up to 5,200 litres (1,352 US gallons) per annum per person!

64   Check to see how much water your toilet uses for each flush. Many older and some modern models use up to 30 per cent more than is needed. A simple way to solve this is to put a clean stone or brick gently into the cistern, making sure that you do not interfere with the mechanical workings.

Many older generation toilets used nine litres per flush. Reducing this to seven litres should not affect the toilet's effectiveness. Thus, if the toilet is used five times per day per person, this would average an environmental saving of up to 3,640 litres (960.4 gallons) per annum per person.

65   Pee in a potty and throw it on the garden or compost heap. Urine can act as an accelerator for composting and the nitrogen contained in it can improve the quality of the resultant fertiliser.

If you pee on average three times a day and your toilet uses 9 litres (2.3 US gallons) per flush, then you can save almost 10,000 litres (2,600 US gallons) of water per person per annum from just not flushing your pee down the drain!

66   Ensure that your washing machine and dishwasher are full before using.

Why waste 70 litres (18.2 US gallons) of water and a kWh of electricity to wash one garment, when it can wash up to five kg (11 lb) of clothes? If you are in the habit of using your machine for single items, you could be wasting the price of a new pair of jeans in energy costs alone every year. Similarly, if washing dishes by hand, only do so when you have enough to merit a bowl-full of hot water.

67   If you like to drink cold water in summer, instead of running the tap for ages until it runs cold, keep a jug or bottle of water in the fridge.

68   Don't use a hose for washing your car.
A hose uses over 30 buckets of water per average wash, whereas you can do a very good job manually with three to five buckets!

69   If you really want a deep soak in the bath, share it with your partner if you have one. A shared soak can be a wonderful way to maintain the romance in your relation-ship and is less damaging to the environment.
An average bath contains 80 litres (20.8 US gallons) of water, so if you share at least one romantic bath a week, you can save the price of a good bottle of champagne per year.

70   If you do not have a garden, retain your bath water to flush the toilet. Simply have a basin beside the bath to transfer the water.
Takes only seconds and means you use no extra water for flushing.

71   Do not flush the toilet after peeing, rather wait for number 2 and do it then.
You can avoid using extra cleaner by giving the toilet a 10 sec-ond rub of the toiletbrush first thing every day.

72   If you have a swimming pool that doesn't use chlo-rine gas, cover the pool whenever it isn't in use.
This reduces water evaporation by between 90 and 95 per cent

and for the average pool you can save up to 7,000 UK gallons (31,850 litres) a year!

Suggestions that cost nothing

73   If you have a rain barrel, use water from it for washing your car. ☐

Alternatively, if you haven't got a rain barrel, you could use the water from your shower or bath.

74   If using a commercial car wash, try and do so at one that recycles its water. ☐

Such car-wash machines reduce the amount of water required by up to 80 per cent, and so should be supported. They cost no more than water-wasting car washes for the driver, but slash the garage owners' water charges.

75   Use old dishwater for soaking used dishes. ☐

Do not throw used dishwater down the sink as soon as you have finished, but rather retain it for soaking used dishes later on, instead of using clean water from the tap. It also means that the heat in the water is also retained in your kitchen as it cools in the sink rather than in the drain.

76   When washing up, use a bowl of clean water to rinse dishes in rather than running the tap constantly. ☐

Running the tap continuously wastes an enormous amount of water. For example, a bowl of water used for rinsing dishes uses about 12 litres (3.1 US gallons) of water, while a running tap uses more than 90 litres (23.4 US gallons) if left running for ten minutes. If the flow is higher, even more water will be wasted.

77   Also use a bowl to wash vegetables instead of simply running the tap. ☐

The bowl will have been filled over ten times if you continu-ously run the tap when one bowl is perfectly sufficient.

78   Throw used dishwater on the garden in summer or during dry spells (presuming that you have switched to biodegradable washing-up liquids already).

Does some good here rather than being wasted down the sink.

79   After you have boiled eggs or vegetables use the enriched water to water your household plants (but wait until it has cooled down!).

Similarly, waste water from your fish tank can be used to water potted plants.

80   Don't cut your grass too short.

Shorter grass uses up more water as it fails to shade the soil as effectively as longer grass.

81   Leave grass cuttings on the lawn in summer.

It acts as moisture-retaining mulch. Dumping grass cuttings, which are mainly composed of water, is unforgivable! It increases the amount of global warming methane emitted by landfill and increases the amount the local authority has to pay for garbage removal. By leaving it on the lawn, the water quickly evaporates and the nutrients are returned to the soil.

82   Grass only needs watering if there is a really prolonged drought, and even then only once a week. When you do water in a drought, give it a good drenching to encourage the roots to go deeper. Allowing your grass to go a little brown during dry spells is not the end of the world. This is a natural phe-nomenon and it will return to its green colour in the hours fol-lowing a shower, and you will appreciate its greenness even more! If you have installed the water-recycling measures, you can avoid even this temporary bout of natural brown grass.

Watering the grass too often can result in the roots remaining on the surface rather than going deeper to where the moisture remains even in most dry spells.

83   If watering garden plants, aim the water at the base of the plants rather than on the foliage.
It is the roots that absorb the water after all, not the leaves! Water left on the leaves simply evaporates.

84   Do your garden watering in the evening.
This allows the water a better chance to soak in to the roots overnight, rather than evaporating in the sunshine with no benefit to the plants.

85   Add the humus from your compost heap to your exposed garden soil.
This increases its water-retention capacity, and so reduces watering needs in summer.

86   Only water trees and shrubs when necessary.
Most trees and shrubs only need watering from when they are first planted until they are established, and thereafter only if there is a severe drought. Frequent and unnecessary watering will prevent the roots from digging deep into the soil, which means they will continue to need hand watering.

87   When watering other plants, only do so according to their individual needs.
When they do need watering, do so thoroughly to encourage deep rooting. Potted plants will probably require more frequent watering, but do ensure that their pots are shaded so the sun doesn't evaporate the water before they can drink it.

88   Parsnips, turnips and onions need watering only very occasionally. Plants grown for their edible leafs such as

spinach, cabbage and lettuce usually require the most frequent watering. Most herbs like the soil to be dry and will only need watering in a prolonged drought once they have been established.

89   If you have to run your hot-water tap for a while before it becomes hot enough to use, save the precious, clean, cold water in a bucket and use for other purposes around the house instead of letting it flow down the plug hole.

You can do this by collecting the cold water in a plastic dish and transferring it to a bucket. You can then fill the dish with the hot water to wash in and it is then very easy to sling the used water on your plants instead of down the drain.

Suggestions that cost a small amount of money

90   Install a water butt attached to your roof guttering down pipe.

An average water butt (which looks like a large barrel) costs only about the price of about six tickets to the cinema and is usually easily installable if you have plastic down pipes from your roof. Ask your local authority or water company if they provide free or cut-price butts. If they don't, ask them why not! While involving a small initial investment, if you pay for water by the meter you will recoup the initial investment over time.

91   If you are refurbishing or laying down a new driveway or footpath, use materials that allow the rainwater to seep down into the water table below, rather than straight into the drain. Bark and wood chippings are often used for footpaths, which are totally biodegradable over time. If you use chippings from your own trees, you can save material costs too.

This not only helps to water nearby plants, but allows the under-ground aquifers to recharge, rather than hastening the return of the water to the sea.

92   If you have to use a hosepipe, get one with a trigger nozzle.

This will cut down the amount of wasted water. For every minute that you save by using the trigger, you can save up to 15 litres (3.9 US gallons) of otherwise wasted water.

93   If you don't have one, see if you can get your water company to install a water meter.

Paying for your water according to how much you use encour-ages efficient use. The average metered home in the UK pays 16 per cent less for its annual supply compared to the average non-metered home, but only one in five homes in Britain have a water meter. Over 90 per cent of homes in the United States have their homes metered. In New York, that figure reaches over 97 per cent.

94   Install spray taps if buying new taps, or see if you can retrofit spray attachments to your current taps.

This costs approximately the price of a good bottle of cham-pagne but saves up to 60 per cent of water used by non-spray taps.

95   Install tap flow regulators.

These are metal restrictors inserted inside the tap, which can reduce the water flow by up to 75 per cent! Can be adjusted to different levels necessary for sink and bath taps.

96   Fix dripping taps as quickly as possible.

A slow dripping tap can leak over 35 litres (9.1 US gallons) per day, which is 12,000 litres (3,120 US gallons) per year down the plughole. It will cost you a small amount of money to fix, instead of significant amounts in lost water.

97   Similarly, fix faulty ball-cock valves to stop your over-flow dripping from your water tanks.

98   Ensure that your water pipes are properly lagged to protect them against frost damage.

Burst pipes can obviously lead to large losses of water, which if metered will add to your repair bill not to mention potential damage to your home. You can lose a massive amount of water this way, especially if you are away on business or holidays. Of course, adequate lagging will also prevent heat from escaping, reducing your energy bills also.

99   Buy a low-flow aerating showerhead.

Low-flow showerheads aerate the water, reducing the amount of water needed, without the person showering noticing any difference. On average, they use approximately 25 litres (6.5 US gallons) per five-minute shower, compared to 50 litres (13 US gallons) for the more traditional showerhead. They cost approximately the price of one bottle of good wine, but if used by a family of four every day it will pay for itself in approximately five months.

100   If your bath or shower is upstairs, install a diverter on the outflow pipe and divert it for watering the garden.

There are gizmos that you can attach to your down pipe that will divert the water into a hose for your garden. They cost only about the price of two bottles of good wine.

101   If you use a shower, buy a large, flat plastic basin in which you can stand while showering.

For the cost of a bowl, this will save all the water which other-wise would have gone down the plughole, and you can use it for a whole range of things around the house from cleaning your sinks to washing your front door! This was done automatically at the yoga centre I went on holidays to in Crete, and we threw the water on the plants in the garden after showering, which added an extra pleasure to the shower! We also use the saved water for flushing the toilet.

102 Install a variable flush control on your toilet.

This ingenious toilet handle regulates the amount of water, so you can use only half the usual quantity for a pee. They are available by mail order and are easily installable; even I was able to do it fairly successfully. They cost about the price of a pair of jeans.

103 If buying a new washing machine or dishwasher, ensure that it is a water-efficient model. Front loading machines are usually more water and energy efficient than top-loading machines. On average, they use 50 litres (13 US gallons) of water less and use less than 50 per cent of the energy per cycle.

It may cost a little extra to start with, but it will save you water and the energy used for heating that water for its entire lifetime.

Suggestions that require a significant capital investment

104 If building a new home, include a large water tank in the foundations.

This can store large amounts of rainwater, which can then be pumped around the home (the pump can be solar powered of course). These tanks were common in Victorian homes. Indeed, I remember a number of the Irish farmhouses that I visited as a boy having large concrete tanks built onto the side of the homes to store rainwater, and so reducing the need for carrying buckets of water from the nearest well.

105 Install a grey-water system in your home.

Black water is the name used for the water contaminated by sewage. Grey water is the term used for all other used water in the home. Grey-water systems clean up used non-wc wastewater eg from your washing machine and bath, and recycle it for non-potable use in the home; for example flushing your toilet. A basic system with a capacity of 180 litres (46.8 US gallons) currently costs approximately the same price as two good-quality washing machines, plus the cost of installation by a plumber. It reduces water consumption by between 30 to 40 per cent. Thus the more of you in the household, the faster the capital investment pays itself back.

106 Install a rain-harvester, and if possible connect it to your toilet.

A rain-harvester is a system that captures the rain falling on your roof, cleans it and diverts it for use in toilets or non-drinking taps. The simple system I installed in my house cost the same as a medium-sized fridge. While being a significant investment, if you pay for metered water, you will recoup the cost over time, depending on your use and local rainfall. When I run out of rainwater for my toilet, I simply turn on the mains supply again. Legally, you must have a system that ensures the rainwater can never enter the mains system. You can find your local rain-harvester installers by searching the web.

107 If you have access to land, buy a new Swedish composting toilet or a book on how to build your own.

Modern composting toilets are quite expensive, costing the equivalent of two good washing machines. They use a very low wattage (6 watts) coil to heat the solid waste and help it to decompose. In four to six weeks you have lovely fertile compost that will enrich your garden. (They have a pipe that leads up to the roof to take away any odours.) For a household of two people who work from home, the economic pay-back period for the investment it would take a minimum of 18 years, but it could be longer in most cases. Of course, the more people who buy them while they are expensive, the faster prices will drop as economies of production kick in. The environmental saving over 37 years would be up to an extraordinary 1,212,120 litres (315,151 US gallons).

Other suggestions

1 _____ □

2 _____ □

3 _____ □

4 _____ □

5 _____ □

_____

	Year 1	Year 2	Year 3	Year 4	Year 5
Suggestions Score (subtotal)					

Chapter 4
Positively Fuelling our Lives

Overuse of oil and other hydrocarbon fuels such as natural gas is leading to climate change, one of our most urgent environmental threats. As temperatures rise and the ice caps melt, millions of people living on islands and low-lying coastal plains are threatened with flooding over the coming century from rising sea waters. Hundreds of billions of pounds will have to be invested in coastal defence measures worldwide. London alone is investing over £4 billion to raise the Thames Barrier flood defences. The Energy Savings Trust in the UK estimate that 180,000 businesses, 1.8 million homes and 3.5 million acres covering 61 per cent of grade-one land in England and Wales are at risk from flooding due to global warming. This would directly affect over 5 million people. The European insurance industry believes that over the next decade, climate change will cost the world economy over $150 billion annually, and that is long before it is predicted to really start kicking in – in about 45 years. Academics at Berkeley University have predicted an annual cost to US agriculture of between 15 to 30 billion dollars if a temperature rise of 5°C occurs by 2050.

Scientists also predict altered weather patterns, with some countries suffering from significantly increased rainfall and storms while others suffer from drought. There is even a threat that the great global ocean currents could be reduced or eliminated. This would be disastrous for the economies of vast sections of the globe. North Eastern Europe, for example, depends on the warm air brought from the Caribbean for its temperate climate and rich agricultural production. The potential consequences for nature are equally devastating.

But climate change is not the only price we are paying for our excessive use of oil and gas. Access to oil has already been at the root of a significant numbers of wars. Western economies received their first major oil shock in the early 1970s when the Organisation for Petroleum Exporting Countries first flexed its muscles on oil prices. It is one of the greatest failures of our political institutions that over 30 years later our economies are still almost as completely fossil-fuel dependent as they were then.

Nuclear energy is leaving an expensive waste disposal problem not only for us and for our children's generation, but also for thousands of years into the future. Stockpiles of radioactive waste have been building up for over 50 years, but no one has come up with a viable and safe solution for their disposal. Nuclear power stations are now also dangerous targets for terrorists, as they weren't designed to withstand airliners potentially crashing into them.

Coal-burning power stations emit significantly more carbon dioxide than even oil or gas-powered stations. Taken together, electric power stations emit over 45 per cent of Australia's CO_2 emissions. The figure is 38 per cent in the US and 28 per cent in the UK. Reducing energy requirements by increasing efficiency, eliminating waste and replacing oil, coal and nuclear energy with renewable fuels are some of the most urgent tasks our generation faces.

When I came back from the Amazon in 1991, I had a dream that my house would be totally energy self-sufficient. My dad had left me some money so I looked into buying a solar-electricity system. However, at the time I could see no way around buying a large number of toxic chemical-based batteries to store the energy created by the solar panels. I thought this really did not make sense. I got on with smaller initiatives instead, such as gradually replacing all my light bulbs with energy-saving bulbs, which use a fifth of the energy for the same amount of light. When I bought a new fridge and washing machine, I ensured we got the most energy efficient products on the market. When I had to replace the back window and door, I replaced them with double glazed versions.

Solar power presented itself to me again when my mother died in 1997 and left me £20,000 pounds. Having only a part-time job at the time (chosen deliberately to allow me the free time to devote to my environmental and political work) and having a £30,000 mortgage, I was faced with a challenging choice. Should I be 'sensible' and pay off the bulk of the mortgage, being in a fairly tenuous employment and financial position, or do I fulfil my dream and try again to install a solar electric system? I chose the latter.

I looked into various solar systems and was put in contact with Martin Cotterell who ran a small company called Sundog. Martin had been a campaigner for Greenpeace before he set up his renewable energy installation company and is a passionate advocate of renewables. He came to my house to assess it for solar potential. He is a tall, thin chap with a wispy red beard and we instantly recognised fellow environmental warriors. He went up on the roof with a strange looking glass-domed technical gizmo which allowed him to plot the solar potential of the roof, taking into account its orientation in relation to the sun and the shadows from the adjoining trees and buildings. Because I have a south-facing roof, and there aren't too many tall buildings beside it, Martin decided a ten-panel system would be viable if I lowered the chimney and the overhanging gable wall. I thought this would be hugely expensive, but one of my local roofers did the necessary building work for a few hundred quid. The exciting news was that the previous antipathy I'd had to the battery-based system had been overtaken by events.

When I had looked into solar power in the early 1990s, everyone had been trying to improve battery capacity and efficiencies. However, Martin told me that the technology now existed to convert the direct current (DC) energy created by the photovoltaic panels to alternating current (AC) energy. AC is the type of electric current used in grid-connected homes. He explained that this meant that I could use the national electricity grid as my battery storage system. During the day in summer when the house would be producing far more electricity than I would use, I would export it to the grid. At night and in the winter, when the roof would be producing none or very little electricity, I would import electricity as normal from the grid, but in theory it would be merely the electricity that I had previously exported. The cost then for the installed system would be about £13,000 (US$23,500 or 20,000).

Up till then, electricity companies had not shown marked enthusiasm for domestic customers doing this. However, when I spoke to the supply contracts negotiator at my electricity company I discovered he was also an enthusiast for renewables. He was really friendly and helpful, but the negotiations were still challenging as it was the first time the company had signed up a private home to supply them with electricity (rather than the usual other way round)! They initially wanted to load a whole set of extra charges onto me, including a second annual charge for selling them electricity, in addition to the annual charge I already paid for buying it off them. They also wanted to charge for testing the installation and an annual hire charge for the export meter.

After a number of months we finally tentatively agreed a package I was happy with. In essence, I would continue to pay my regular domestic electricity charge of 6.8p per unit as normal and they would pay me the grid price at the time of 2.8p per unit but with no extra charges for the privilege of selling my electricity to them. However, they rang me a few days later and reversed all the tentatively agreed positions. I don't know what happened: the negotiator probably had to refer the package to the management above him who feared a precedent being set. The negotiations had been friendly up to this point, but I felt I had to be firm and use what I could to ensure a good precedent was set. I gently intimated that I might go to the press and state that they were being obstructive in helping this new technology get off the ground. I was delighted to get a phone call just a few days later confirming the package as originally agreed without any of the extra charges, if I signed up for three years. This I duly did, and the contract was signed soon after, establishing a positive precedent for all those who followed. My electricity company had signed up their first domestic electricity supplier rather than customer. Martin Cotterell was stunned. He said as far as he knew, no one had managed to get a major electricity supplier to sign a metered supply contract from a private domestic home before. This was truly good news for the renewable energy community.

At the same time as I was negotiating this I was sorting out planning permission for the installation of the solar panels on the roof, as a precedent had to be set there too. I wanted to avoid planning charges, if at all possible, as again that would bite into the economic arguments for installing solar power. A local family had wanted to install a solar water-heating system, but the local council insisted it needed planning permission, and they came to me seeking advice in the previous year. I sought legal advice in turn from the local council's solicitor, which as an elected councillor at that time I was able to do. They stated that as the alterations did not change the roofline and the building was not in a conservation area, they could be exempted from planning permission following a written request. So when it came to sort out the planning situation for my own solar-electricity system, the first private solar-powered house to be grid connected in London, I wrote seeking an exemption. I explained that the panels did not alter the roofline of the house, could not be seen from the street as they were on the rear roof elevation and my home was not listed nor was it in a conservation area. I was delighted when a couple of weeks later I received the necessary letter of exemption. I had managed another first with the system.

Martin then forged ahead with the installation. A government energy minister had recently appeared on television stating that retrofitting solar-electricity systems on older houses was impossible. Well, Martin soon proved him wrong, as he quickly and successfully installed the ten-panel system on the rear roof of my 1840s two-up/two-down terraced cottage. It was also the first system in the country to use individual inverters for each solar panel. These new inverters had just been brought on the market in the Netherlands. They meant that if a shadow from a tree or building fell on one panel, the flow of electricity from all the panels wasn't halted, as it is if only one inverter is being used for the entire array of panels.

The solar panels have now been installed for over five years without any hitches. At the end of my three-year contract, I contacted the electricity company about renewing my supply contract. They offered not only to give me reverse metering, but also to give me the full new green premium price they had introduced for consumers who wished to buy green electricity. Reverse metering is where they pay you what you pay them, symbolised by a meter going backwards when you are exporting.

This has meant that my annual invoice to London Electricity for electricity exported to them has jumped from the fairly miserable £17 to the more respectable £40. At least now I can dine out for two on the income! As I have been living alone for the last few years, I have found that I am exporting roughly the same amount of electricity over the year as I am importing. In summer I often export over four times what I am importing but in winter I am producing less than ten per cent.

Reductions in VAT, taken with grants and the reduction in costs of the systems themselves, means that a similar solar panel system to mine now costs in the region of £6,000 (US$11,000 or 9,500), a saving of 50 per cent. The only reason that it is not far cheaper, according to a report by KPMG, is that there is not a production facility yet built that is big enough to produce solar panels in sufficient numbers to enable the price to collapse. However, the technology is already competitive with oil if only governments would remove market blockages. We need to create a demand to justify such plants, and we need governments to form partnerships to enable them to be built. It is estimated that the capital costs for one plant would be in the region of £300 million ($530 million). This is a fraction of the cost of the many oil wars that are continually waged in the Middle East, or of the subsidies poured by many governments into the nuclear industry.

I am currently working on another renewable energy project for my home. I wanted to produce more of my own electricity in winter, so I decided to look into installing a grid-connected micro-windmill. I contacted Martin Cotterell last summer and again, surprisingly, he said he was aware of no one who had done such a thing. Up to now, most windmills had been commercial, and generally in rural or maritime areas. He said that there was a possibility that a certain type of inverter might work with a micro-windmill to produce AC electricity that would be exportable to the grid. He promised to try and see if he could get some of his contacts to check it out. Meanwhile, I contacted my electricity company to let them know of my plans and this time there were no negotiations to go through. They simply said that they would be delighted to buy the wind energy from me at the same premium price that they were paying me for the solar electricity.

Then it was off to the council planning department again. This time it was they who proved to be the challenge. They decided that I needed full planning permission for the installation and would have to pay a fee. This annoyed me: there are ugly satellite dishes everywhere that require no planning permission but do no good for the environment! However after the initial disappointment, I had to agree that planning permission was essential as it ensures that any such development would not cause a disturbance for my neighbours. After petitioning my neighbours and submitting the application twice, the council agreed permission. The British Wind Energy Association says it is the first such successful application they are aware of.

Unfortunately, the inverter that Martin had been hoping to use had failed its government technical tests and the windmill we had intended to use had been reported as being noisy. I didn't want to risk the reputation of renewable energy technology on such a danger (not to mind my own relationship with my neighbours). So it was back to the drawing board to search for the right equipment. We are currently looking at three different British-made micro-windmills, which are rated between 100 and 750 watts. Martin sent the same Dutch inverter that we had used for the solar panels to a wind company that he knew of, to see if it would be suitable for the task we had in mind. They were enthusiastic about this as it meant that it could open up a potential new market for their windmills. As I write, they are currently acting like a couple of enthusiastic university undergraduates communicating back and forth to see if the equipment will deliver what we need it to do in a domestic setting. Hopefully, this will be sorted out soon. I am really looking forward to seeing a windmill whirring on my gable wall, when I turn into my street on my way home.

Having installed my own solar electric system at home, I then started working on the voluntary groups of which I am a member. I persuaded the national membership organisation of which I am a board member to switch its energy supplier for our national headquarters to an electricity company that sourced all of its electricity from renewable sources. This resulted in a £4,000 cut in our annual electricity costs, as we had not re-tendered following deregulation in the electricity market a few years previously. We also benefited from not having to pay the climate-change levy on electricity supplied to commercial premises. I then contacted this renewable energy electricity company to see if they would be interested in exploring the possibility of setting up an affinity scheme for our organisation's 70,000 members spread across the country. They said that they had done no such deals to date but would be very interested.

As a result, our organisation's members can now sign up for renewable electricity supplies for their own homes via our website. They need to have a previous electricity bill from their current electricity supplier to hand as the registering process requires a couple of numbers from the bill. But once the online form is filled in, the renewable electricity company carries out all the rest of the process of informing their current supplier and changing their supply automatically over to 100 per cent renewable energy. There is a premium of ten per cent on top of the usual bill if it is a domestic bill. This means roughly the cost of a couple of packets of crisps per week for clean energy. In my view this is a real bargain. Can you really look in a child's eyes and say it is not worth the investment for their future? I think this is another good example of how by putting your own home in order, you are then better equipped to argue more effectively for greater change out in the wider world.

About 21 per cent of US and 30 per cent of the UK's total energy consumption is used by domestic households. This means that how we use energy in our own homes can make a significant impact on our country's greenhouse-gas emissions. The average three-person home is estimated by Friends of the Earth to emit over five tons of CO_2 from their electricity and gas use alone. In the UK, British Gas estimates that the public waste almost £5 billion of energy every year, whereas the government estimates that the economy as a whole wastes up to £12 billion per year. This is equivalent to 30 per cent of all energy used!

The table below gives you an idea of the amount of electricity various household products use per hour. It is compiled from a random selection of products in a major department store, so you will be able to find individual items that use more or less electricity depending on their efficiency rating, but the list will help you understand the relative energy consequences of using different appliances. One point to remember is that while an appliance may have a low wattage, if it is on for significant amounts of time it may over a year be a far higher consumer of electricity, giving it a higher environmental cost overall than a high wattage utensil on for short periods of time.

Product	Wattage
Electric cooking range	12,000
Electric immersion heater	3–9,000
Clothes dryer	5,000
Rapid boil kettle	3,000
Electric cooker	2,650

Cordless kettle	2,200
Steam iron	2,000
Electric vacuum cleaner	1,800
Regular kettle	1,700
Electric lawn mower	1,600
Electric toaster (4 slice)	1,500
Sandwich toaster	1,500
Home cappucino maker	1,400
Dishwasher	1,300
Hair dryer	1,100
Electric curler	1,000
Electric toaster (2 slice)	1,000
Electric heater	1,000
Microwave oven	1,000
Non-steam traditional iron	900
Washing machine	600
Food blenders	500

Electric hedge trimmer	450
Home cinema system	450
Food mixer	300
Electric bicycle	200
Traditional television	130
Regular lightbulb	100
Small hi-fi system	95
Fridge freezer	90
LCD Television	45
Freezer	35
Energy-saving lightbulb (100 W equivalent)	20
Electric toothbrush charger	2

The average household electricity bill in the UK is currently just above £300, while in the US it is about $870 per annum. Per capita consumption in the US is approximately 12,000 kWh, while in Canada with its colder climate it is about 15,000 kWh. Similar variations also occur in Europe, where electricity consumption varies from the enormous per capita consumptions in the Nordic countries of Norway and Sweden of 24,000 kWh and 15,000 kWh respectively, to the very low per capita consumptions of below 3,000 kWh in the former east-European countires. France, Germany and the UK each average 6,000 kWh per person. The US emits over five times the average worldwide greenhouse gas emissions, while in the UK we emit over twice the global average. There is therefore a moral imperative on those of us who live in developed countries to take a greater share of the burden for reducing global-warming emissions.

I hope this chapter will give you some incentive to reduce *your* CO_2 emissions. Look through the list of suggestions below and see if you can start putting more of them into practice. I am sure you will find that there are some that you are already doing. Remember that the more emissions that we save in our generation, the lower the price the next generation will have to pay. I know for sake of the peace of my conscience I do not want to use energy with a price tag that our kids will end up paying for, whether it is disposing of our nuclear waste or paying for future climate-change disasters. Today is as good a day as any to begin!

How to score

3   if you do the suggestion nearly all the time

2   if you do it occasionally or fairly often

1   if you hardly ever do it

0   if you never do it

Suggestions that save you money

108 Fill the electric kettle only with the number of mugs of water that you are likely to use. Why pay for boiling enough water for people who are not there, when you are having a nice cup of tea for one? If you keep a water jug by the kettle, you can easily fill the kettle with the exact amount you need to boil.

To boil the water for one cup of coffee takes my 2,400 watt kettle one minute. To boil a full kettle (equivalent to nine mugs of coffee) takes it five and a half minutes. The energy wasted boiling the unwanted water is enough to run my energy saving (20W = 100W equivalent) light bulb for nine hours!

109 Do not forget that a covered kettle or pan boils almost six per cent faster.

Covering the kettle not only saves money but also you don't have to wait as long!

110 Turn down the heat under saucepans once they have reached boiling point.

Most of the heat energy used in boiling vegetables is for bring-ing the water to the boil. After that, they require very little energy to keep them bubbling.

111 Ensure that pans are on the right sized ring if you use an electric cooker. Or if you use a gas cooker, that the gas is not wasted by being so high it burns up the side of the pan.

Having the gas burning up along the outside of a pan instead of just under it or having a small pan on a large electric ring wastes energy pointlessly.

112 If boiling potatoes, boil enough for more than one meal.

That way they can then be used on following days for roasting, frying, mashing etc which uses less energy.

113 If roasting meat (or a nut-roast), roast the potatoes and vegetables too.

This thus uses the oven to maximum efficiency. Why use energy to boil them when you can roast them using no extra energy?

114 Avoid opening the over door to check on cooking food.

You lose over 20 per cent of the heat in the oven each time you open it, which means it then has to work harder to replace the lost heat and takes longer to cook your food.

115 Turn off the oven ten minutes before the food is due to be cooked.

The heat in the oven will finish the cooking. Some experimental ovens are so well insulated that they need only to be heated to the required temperature and then turned off!

116 If buying a new gas oven, buy one with electric ignition for lighting the gas.

If you choose one with a gas pilot light, it will be burning gas for the entire lifetime of the appliance and you will be paying for that lifetime's waste of gas!

117 Regularly defrost your fridge if it does not do so automatically.

The thicker the frost the harder the motor works, the more energy it wastes. Maximum frost thickness should be 6 mm (a quarter of an inch).

118 Vacuum clean the condenser coils at the back of your fridge twice a year (if it isn't a no-clean condenser model).

Remember to unplug it first! When finished, don't place the fridge flush with the wall, but allow the condensers space to work efficiently by allowing the expelled heat to dissipate. This can save you up to the price of a couple of pairs of jeans every year in electricity, depending on the size of your fridge.

119 Do not put hot food into or on a fridge. Allow it to cool to room temperature first and then place it in the fridge.

This is because the fridge uses more energy to cool the food down, rather than simply keeping it cool.

120 If defrosting something from your freezer, try moving it from the freezer to the fridge the night before.
The cooling energy invested in the iced product is recycled in the fridge reducing the need to use energy to cool the fridge.

121 Ensure that you defrost food before cooking.
Thawing can reduce the cooking time of frozen products by up to 55 per cent. For example, it takes 25 minutes to cook an oven-ready unfrozen quiche, while it takes 45 minutes to cook from frozen. As ovens are large users of electricity this is quite a significant saving.

122 If you have a freezer in your fridge, ask yourself whether you really need a full-size freezer in addition.
Remember, from the day you turn it on, the freezer will be turned on for every minute of every year it is in your home, which for even a low-energy, 35 watt freezer equals the cost of a pair of new jeans of electricity per year to run it.

123 If you have to have a dishwasher, check to see if the heating element is set too high.
Equally good washing can often be achieved at a lower temperature to the one set. You don't hand-wash dishes in boiling water do you?

124 Do not use your dishwasher's ware-drying programme.
Dishes dry in the air in a very short time. Programme your machine to turn off at the end of the last rinse cycle and leave the door ajar to allow them to dry naturally.

125 Only use the 'rinse hold' in a dishwasher programme if absolutely necessary.

This wastes up to an extra 6 gallons or 23 litres of precious hot water.

126 Do not use your dishwasher or washing machine unless they are reasonably full. ☐

Using a washing machine or dishwasher to wash just a few articles is really environmentally expensive in water, heat and detergent.

127 Ensure you use the appropriate temperature on your washing machine for your clothes. Many people wash their coloured clothes at far too high a temperature. This not only wastes energy but fades the colour of clothes faster. ☐

A wash at 60°C (140°F) uses over 30 per cent more electricity than a wash at 40°C (104°F). Water that is at a temperature of 30–40°C (86–104°F) is more than hot enough for coloured clothes.

128 Ensure also that you are using the appropriate wash cycle on your machine for coloured clothes. ☐

A white wash programme is significantly longer and uses far more energy.

129 Avoid buying too many white clothes and bed linen. ☐

They need very high temperatures to get them shining white and often require some form of bleaching which coloureds do not.

130 Use a natural option rather than a tumble dryer if at all possible. ☐

Tumble dryers are one of the highest energy consumers among domestic appliances. Dry clothes outdoors if you can, or indoors using a clothes-horse and allow them to dry in their own time a safe distance from the radiator.

131 If you feel you have to use a tumble dryer, ensure that your clothes are well wrung out or spun in the washing machine first. ☐

The mechanical energy used in spinning is more efficient than the heat energy used in the electric clothes dryer.

132   Clean out the tumble dryer's lint tray after each use.
A clogged up lint tray will cause the machine to use more energy.

133   If buying a new iron, buy a non-steam iron and use a water handspray instead.
Steam irons can use more than 1,000 watts more electricity per hour than non-steam irons, yet with a handspray the same effect can be achieved. Traditional non-steam irons are also significantly cheaper to buy.

134   Use your kitchen and bathroom air extractor fans only when absolutely necessary.
They not only use energy themselves but can whisk your entire home's warm air out in just under an hour, pointlessly requiring your heating system to heat it up all over again unnecessarily.

135   Use a shower rather than a bath to save energy.
This saves energy as an average three-minute shower uses 30 litres (7.8 US gallons) of water whereas a bath uses between 80 and 200 litres (between 20.8 and 52 US gallons). Remember you also save on the water costs as well as the heating.

136   Never allow the hot-water tap to run while shaving. Run the amount you want into a bowl and when finished throw it on your garden or plants.
It really does not make sense to heat water and then pour that heat down the sink needlessly.

137   Ensure your hot water cylinder isn't set at too high a temperature.

If the water in your tap comes out scalding hot and you need to add cold water, then the setting is too high. Sixty degrees should be adequate for most of your needs. Water heating is one of the most energy intensive processes in your home, and to heat water to a temperature that then needs to be cooled with cold water is illogical.

138 If you are away for more than a day, remember to turn off your electric water heater if you have one.

As electric water immersion-heaters use between 3,000 and 9,000 watts, this is really worth doing in economic as well as environmental terms. Using 3,000 watts for 24 hours costs about the price of a bottle of wine, and if left on while away for a two-week holiday would cost the price of two new pairs of jeans for absolutely nothing.

139 Do not leave appliances with remote controls on stand-by.

Some older models use up to 100 per cent of their full-use energy in stand-by mode, so instead of paying for the couple of hours that you use the television, you could be paying for it being on all day, every day, every year you own it! It is estimated that 5 to 15 per cent of household electricity consumption worldwide is wasted on stand-by mode. With US households it is estimated that stand-by waste costs over $5 billion in electricity a year. Over £150 million pounds worth of electricity is wasted each year in the UK simply keeping televisions and VCRs on stand-by. If we could eliminate this waste, we could close over one in 20 electricity power stations in the UK alone! You can find out from your machine manufacturer about how much energy your machine is using in stand-by. The Organisation for Economic Co-operation and Developement (OECD) estimates that more than two out of every hundred power stations in western Europe could be closed if stand-by electricity wastage was eliminated.

140 Turn off your mobile phone charger at the wall when not using it.

Many such chargers still draw electricity even when not charging. Check with your manufacturer. If it uses five watts an hour and is left on unnecessarily all year round, it can use up to 42 kilowatt hours per year!

141 Turn off the black-box adaptors that are attached to your various TV, VCR, computers, modems etc when not in use.

Again, these continue to use energy even when the machine is not being used. This, together with wasted stand-by energy, is called vulture consumption. If you put your hand on a black-box adapter it will often be quite hot, which shows just how much energy they burn up. It will be small – maybe three to four watts per hour – but, if your home has 12 of these boxes burning away all the time, they can use approximately the cost of a new pair of jeans in electricity per year. This is equivalent to three energy-saving light bulbs being on unnecessarily all day long, every day, all year round.

142 Place your central heating thermostat on an inner wall.

This provides you with a more accurate reading of your room temperature, so avoiding increasing the central-heating temperature setting unnecessarily.

143 Closed curtains or wooden window shutters keep the sun's heat out during the day in summer and the home's heat in during the evenings in winter.

This helps reduce heating and air-conditioning costs.

144 Keep your south-facing windows clean.

In winter this will maximise free heating of your home by the sun.

145 Set the thermostat at a level where you are comfortable

in winter with a reasonable amount of clothes on – around 17 to 19°C/64 to 67°F.

Each degree you lower the temperature will save around five per cent of your heating costs. Don't reduce temperatures below what is comfortable – especially if you have vulnerable members of the household, eg children, the elderly or disabled. We want to save the planet, not make our families ill! (That applies to raising the temperature too high also, as that can make them susceptible to colds etc.)

146 Programme your central heating to go off when asleep (making sure you have enough bedclothing in winter to keep cosy).

Programming it to turn itself off 30 minutes before you go to sleep and on 30 minutes before you get up is the recommended pattern. This can save you up to seven hours of wasted heating energy every night during winter.

147 Place your settees and other seating against inside walls where possible.

This will allow you to escape drafts, so you will be warm at a lower temperature setting of the central heating.

148 Heat/cool only the rooms that you are using. Close doors to unused rooms.

After all why pay to heat four rooms when you are only using two? Don't close your air vents if you have gas appliances, however, as they may be essential for their safe operation.

149 Keep your cupboard and closet doors closed.

Your pots and pans do not need central heating, do they?

150 If you have a fireplace that you never use, consider plugging it up.

This will prevent all your precious central heating escaping up the flue. Do not do this if the flue is used for essential gas-fire ventilation etc.

151   Close fireplace dampers when the fire is not lit in winter. ☐
Stops the cold draft up the chimney wasting all your precious central heating.

152   Only turn your car air-conditioning on when really necessary. ☐
Air-conditioning significantly increases the amount of fuel used by the car, adding an extra 100 litres (26 US gallons) per annum to the average car fuel consumption in countries with temperate climates. Remember every litre of gasoline burnt equals two kg of CO_2 emitted into the atmosphere.

153   If you smoke cigarettes, adopt an energy smart routine. ☐
The average smoker uses up to 50 per cent more energy in their homes than a non-smoker. This is because they tend to have the windows open to get rid of the smell. In winter this means significantly larger heating bills as you are paying not only to heat your home but the outside environment as well! Smoking outside is probably the most environmentally friendly way of smoking and still retaining a habitable home, but not if you leave the door open after you. Or you could smoke in a lightly-used room with the door shut. If you turn off the radiator before opening the window to let the smoke out, it would waste less energy.

Suggestions that cost nothing

154 Take the Earth Summit pledge that commits you to turning the lights and heating off in all rooms that you aren't using. ☐

It costs nothing, and once you take it and observe it for a while you'll become allergic to leaving lights and heating on in rooms that are not in use.

155 Don't have more lights on in a room than are needed.

My bathroom had two lights that turned on automatically when you entered the room. When I removed the second light, the room was still well lit with the one light so I halved the cost of lighting the room from then on with just one action!

156 If buying new light fittings, ensure that energy-saving bulbs can be fitted to them.

Energy-saving light bulbs are often thicker at the bayonet end, requiring more space at the point that they are connected to the fitting than traditional bulbs. If you do this, you won't be stuck with fittings that have to use energy-wasting bulbs for their entire lifetime.

157 Do not leave outside lights on unnecessarily.

After all, the cat can see in the dark, so why waste lighting when no one is there?

158 If installing new outside lighting, use sensor lights that come on only when people are present.

Reduces wasted electricity.

159 If you have a gas furnace, ensure it has a free flow of air from the outside.

This will help ensure efficient and safe operation.

160 Regularly bleed trapped air from your hot-water central heating radiators.

Trapped air prevents the radiator from working properly, which means the heat generated by the boiler does not get into the room and is wasted.

161 Buy sustainably-produced local charcoal.

The UK, for example, imports over 60,000 tonnes of charcoal every year. Much of it comes from South-east Asia and from Central and South American threatened rainforests. Buying domestically-produced charcoal reduces transport miles and can also help to create a domestic market for the tree timber that arises from your local council's street and park trees. Up until now nearly all of this has been disposed of in the waste stream instead of being put to a useful purpose.

Suggestions that cost a small amount extra

162 Switch your household electricity supply to a renewable supplier if available. Check it out on the web.

The renewable electricity supply company Good Energy was judged the best renewable-electricity supplier in the UK for two years in a row (2001 and 2002 by Friends of the Earth). All I had to do to sign up was fill in my account details from my old supplier online, and Good Energy did the rest. They charge a 10 per cent premium on non-renewable energy, which works out at a couple of packets of crisps per week for the average family. I think this is a bargain for a clear conscience about where one's electricity is coming from! See the resources at the back of this book for EU and US web contacts for green energy suppliers.

163 If buying a new washing machine, dish washer or vacuum cleaner check the energy rating of the product to ensure it is the most energy-efficient available. These are often on the label in the store. Consumer magazines now often provide advice on the best environmental buys.

These products will usually cost a little extra but will save energy for their entire lifetime.

164 The same applies to fridges and fridge-freezers.

Their range of annual electricity consumption can be from 220 kWh to nearly 2,000 kWh for larger old-fashioned fridge-freezers! It depends on the size and energy efficiency of the fridge. As fridges and freezers are on continuously from the day you bring them home, it is crucial that you buy the most efficient. Check the energy ratings supplied by the manufacturer.

165 Again, when replacing your water heater or central-heating boiler, ensure that you install the most energy efficient model on the market.

Water heating is one of the most energy-intensive activities in your home.

166 Have your water heater and central-heating boiler regularly maintained if they are gas or oil fired.

As well as using energy more efficiently, a well-maintained water heater is also of course safer.

167 If buying a new electric oven, consider buying a fan-forced oven.

These are up to a third faster than conventional ovens so save up to a third of the electricity used. They also avoid the need for pre-heating the oven, making them even more efficient; but remember to cut your cooking time when reading recipe instructions.

168 Ensure that the seals on your fridge and oven are intact and repair them if damaged.

Damaged seals mean that the cold or hot air you are paying for is simply leaking out.

169 If buying new cooking pots, buy a stack-steamer.

These are pots designed to stack on top of each other and can cook almost an entire meal on one stove ring, thus saving the expense of using three rings. Prices start from about the price of a pair of jeans upwards depending on quality.

170 Buy a pressure cooker, which uses far less time and energy for cooking food than conventional cookers.

Pressure cookers cost between approximately three to four times the cost of a good quality saucepan, but they use less than 50 per cent of the energy of traditional cooking methods, so will save you money in the long run.

171 Check out with your manufacturer or supplier to see if a Savaplug is appropriate for your fridge.

This is a small gadget that sends power to the fridge in short bursts, rather than continuously, and can save up to 20 per cent of your fridge's annual running costs. You put your fridge plug into the Savaplug, which then plugs into the wall socket.

172 If your single glazed windows are not ready for replacing or if you cannot afford double-glazing, you can get strong, see-through plastic that you can attach to your windows in winter. An even cheaper option is to apply plastic wrap to the inside of your window frames with a hairdryer. If your house uses gas appliances, make sure that you have adequate ventilation before implementing this measure.

40 metres (43.6 yards) of plastic wrap costs only about the price of three packets of crisps!

173 Ensure that all windows and doors have their gaps insulated.

Strip insulation for windows and doors costs only the price of a bottle of wine per metre and as you can lose up to 10 per cent of your heating through such gaps, this is probably one of the easiest and cheapest methods of saving energy. The strips usually come as self-adhesive, so all you have to do is cut the tape to size and stick it on, once the surface it is being applied to is clean and dry.

174 If you are buying new curtains, make sure that they are well lined and as thick as possible.

The thicker and more insulating they are the more they keep you warm and cosy.

175 Fit energy-saving bulbs in all relevant light sockets.

These bulbs use one fifth of the energy of old fashioned incandescent bulbs and last up to ten times longer. For example, a 20-watt, energy-saving bulb provides the equivalent of a 100-watt, non-energy-saving bulb. Thus over its 10,000 hour lifespan it uses 200,000 watt-hours of electricity instead of one million watt-hours! This roughly means a saving of over two pairs of jeans per bulb/lifetime use in electricity alone. Top quality 20-watt bulbs cost approximately the same as a good bottle of wine but there are now some 15-watt bulbs that cost only the price of a good imported beer. British Gas and other utilities often have special offers for energy-saving bulbs where they sell them at very low prices. Check to see if any utilities in your area have such special energy-saving offers by checking their websites or contacting their customer information lines.

176 If there is a gap under the outside doors, attach a door sweep.

An easily applied door sweep, which is a band of bristles that sweeps the floor as you close it and blocks the drafts, costs about the price of two bottles of wine. You can lose a huge amount of energy if there is a significant gap under your outer doors, so ensure that they are sorted.

177 Draughty letterboxes can lead to an expensive loss of heat. Ensure yours is draught proof. ☐

Replacing a draughty letterbox pays for itself in no time as they cost only about the same as a half litre of wine.

178 If you have an electric hot-water tank, ensure that it has a good quality lagging-jacket. Do not lag gas boilers: it can be dangerous! ☐

Remember that your electric hot-water cylinder will undoubtedly be one of the largest energy users in your home. They use between 3,000 and 9,000 watts per hour!! A lagging jacket costs only the equivalent of a couple of bottles of wine, but cuts up to 75 per cent of your annual hot-water costs, as the energy is retained as hot water rather than lost to the surrounding air. Thus, the jacket will repay itself in months. If you choose only one thing from this list of energy suggestions to implement, please consider doing this one if you have an electric immersion heater.

179 Ensure that the hot-water pipes from your boiler are insulated, especially if it is located outside the living area such as in the garage. ☐

You are paying for the energy to provide hot water from your taps, not to heat the air along the way. Lagging insulation costs only between one and two packets of crisps per metre.

180 If you have an electric boiler, ensure that you buy an electric timer, so that you have hot water only when you want it. ☐

There is no point in paying for having hot water available all day when you are at work and all night when you are asleep. Even if you are not using the hot water, the boiler still uses electricity to keep the water hot. A timer can cost as little as a bottle of wine and pays for itself in just a few months in saved energy costs.

181 Ensure your central heating is off when you are away from home.

You can get programmable thermostats that allow you to pro-gramme your heating for the week, but which are easily man-ually overridden when going away on holiday or if you do not need it during a normal week.

182 Attach water spray saving attachments to your hot-water taps as well as your cold-water taps.

This saves your heating bills as well as your water bills, as it reduces the amount of hot water wasted.

183 Install radiator reflector foil behind your radiators.

This reflects the heat you pay for back into the room, rather than wasting it on heating the street outside, through your walls.

184 If you do not live in a smoke-free zone and have an open fire, you can buy a log maker that makes compact logs out of old newspapers.

One newspaper makes one log. They only cost approximately the price of a pair of jeans, and so make sense for a lifetime's log making without having your own trees. You simply soak the paper in water and the log maker shapes it into a log.

185 When buying services or holidays, consider buying them through organisations that are signed up to carbon offset schemes like Climate Care (UK), Carbon Counter (US) or Climate Partners (Canada).

This type of scheme means that if you buy such items as a mortgage, holiday, car-breakdown service, phone-line, bank loan, car hire etc through a company signed up to the scheme, then they invest a set figure in a project that reduces global CO_2 by an amount generated by your purchase. The services offered by the different schemes vary from country to country. The best way of finding your local scheme is to type in 'carbon offset scheme + your country' into a web search engine.

186 You can also offset your own individual CO_2 emissions the easy way by making an individual donation to a CO_2 offset programme, rather than depending on a company to do it for you.

This service means that you can calculate how much CO_2 for example would be used in your return flight from London to Los Angeles (about 2.6 tonnes of CO_2 per person emitted). There is usually an easy-to-use calculator on the offset programme's website. You can then pay a donation to be invested in reducing that amount of CO_2 from the environment through tree planting, energy efficiency or renewable energy schemes online. The Climate Care scheme will accept payments in dollars, Euros and pounds sterling from anywhere in the world, but you should check whether there is a scheme operating in your country first.

187 If you are thinking of changing your bank, telephone company etc consider choosing a company that is environmentally aware such as the Phone Co-op or Co-operative Bank in the UK.

They donate to CO_2 offset schemes and the Co-operative Bank has won prizes for the environmental auditing of its activities.

188 If buying a new radio, consider the latest generation of wind-up radios, which for a little effort provide up to an hour of play time.

These range from the price of a cheap pair of new jeans for a cheap basic wind-up radio to the equivalent of an expensive pair of jeans for the latest, deluxe, combined solar/wind-up technology, which also have long wave stations.

189 If buying a new torch, also consider the newest generation of solar or wind-up torches.

Wind-up torches are available on the net for the price of a new pair of jeans. Sixty seconds of winding can give 16 minutes of light.

190 There are now solar mobile phone rechargers or for those of you who like cycling there are cycle mobile phone rechargers!

A cycle recharger that will recharge your mobile on your way to work costs the price of a pair of jeans on the web, whereas a solar phone recharger is a bit pricier.

191 If you have a bicycle, install a dynamo for your lights instead of using toxic batteries, or use rechargeable batteries.

There are now dynamo sets available that continue lighting for up to five minutes after you stop cycling.

192 When fitting a new water heating or central-heating system ensure that you use the fuel that causes the least carbon dioxide emissions.

Gas is the best, with emissions of 194g/kWh, and then comes oil with 270g/kWh and coal with 317g/kWh. The worst is electricity with 511g/kWh – the crucial exception is of course electricity from renewable sources, which is the lowest carbon-dioxide emitter.

Suggestions that require a significant capital investment

193 Ensure that your roof is properly insulated.

The cost of loft insulation for a three-bedroom, semi-detached home costs about the same price as a cheap washing machine. In the UK, British Gas estimates that proper insulation will save its installation costs in saved energy in about two and a half years. Look out for special offers from some utilities during the summer period.

194 Similarly, ensure that your walls are properly insulated. □

Installing cavity wall insulation can cost about the same as insulating your roof space, ie the cost of a cheap washing machine, but it repays itself in heat saved in about five years.

195 Install a micro-hydro electricity generator if you have a stream or river on your property. □

A small, battery-charging micro-hydro system costs from about the price of a good quality washing machine upwards, depending on the size required. I know someone who has installed one in a stream on his Welsh hill farm and produces so much electricity in winter that he uses the excess to heat his cow barn!

196 Install a small domestic windmill, or even a larger commercial-sized one if you live in the countryside. Small, 100-watt-rated DC windmills start out at the price of a cheap washing machine. □

Many farmers are making a significant income from the installation of commercial wind generators on their land. Even one large turbine can provide a nice little earner for very little work. Contact the American or British Wind Energy Association for information on how to go about it or whether it might work in your area. For other countries, check the European Wind Energy Association's website, which has a database of Wind Energy Associations around the world, which may be able to provide you with information specific to the country you live in.

197 Install solar photovoltaic panels on your roof. These panels produce renewable energy by converting the sun's energy into electricity. □

The Solar Electric Power Association website is a good place to *start your research in the United States. An installed system in the UK will now cost from about £6,000 (US$11,000 or 8,500) upwards when you include the 50-per-cent government grants that are now often available. Contact the Energy Savings Trust for information on these grants in the UK. Many electricity companies now allow you to export excess production to the national electricity grid during the day and will pay you for it. This generates a very modest income and means that you do not need an expensive battery system in your home, as the national grid acts as your battery store. This is because you can export to the grid during the day when you are not at home and import it at night when you need the electricity and there is no sunshine to power your solar panels. These systems are not competitive with your commercial electricity supplier yet, but the more people who buy them, the lower the cost will become. Greenpeace has produced a report that says once mass production efficiencies kick in, solar electricity will be competitive with current oil prices.*

198   If you are replacing any windows or doors that have windows, ensure that you install double-glazed units but avoid the toxic PVC or energy-intensive aluminium options. Choose double-glazed wooden doors and windows instead with wood from sustainable sources.

Up to 25 per cent of your space heating can be lost through badly insulated windows. You can save up to the price of two pairs of jeans per annum if your windows are properly insulated.

199   Install thermal shutters on your windows.

These will keep heat out in summer and in during the winter.

200   If you have an Aga, wood stove or other type of cooking range, fit an air fan above them.

These will move the hot air to cooler parts of the home, which can remove the need for further heating in these areas.

201 If fitting a new hot-water heating system, ensure that it is the latest and most efficient model.

Systems that instantly heat what is required rather than waste energy preheating the hot water and storing it are preferable if a solar system is not practical or affordable.

202 If you have an old central-heating boiler replace it with the latest condensing boilers.

The latest generation of condensing, gas central-heating boilers are up to 37 per cent more efficient than those put in 15 years ago and are up to 12-per-cent more efficient than modern, non-condensing boilers. According to British Gas, if you replace an old boiler with the latest condensing boiler you could in a three-bedroom property save up to £2,000 (US$3,500 or 2,800) over the 15-year lifespan of the system.

203 If you have a large home with a large family, install a waste water heat-recovery system.

This rescues the heat you have paid for from the water as it leaves your home after being used and recycles it in your home.

204 Install a solar water-heating system, which are in many climates now competitive with fossil fuel heated systems.

Over a million domestic solar water-heating systems have already been installed in the United States alone. A basic system can cost from about US$2,000 upwards. Energy Source Guides has a very comprehensive website listing all solar water-heating supply businesses in the United States in order of state by state — www.energy.sourceguides.com. This website is also very useful for other renewable energy companies across the US. The UK Government has set up a scheme called Clear Skies, which provides £500 grants for the installation of solar water-heating systems in domestic homes. A fully installed solar water-heating system costs between £2,300 and £4,000 (3–6,000) in the UK but costs can be substantially reduced by installing your own. Clubs teaching people how to do this themselves are springing up across the UK. Additional grants of up to £500 are available from some London borough councils, reducing the installation cost to £1,300 depending on where you live. Payback periods for the investment are estimated to be between 7 and 15 years depending on the number of users etc. It can provide up to 90 per cent of your hot-water needs in summer and up to 30 per cent even in winter. These figures are based on a temperate climate and will vary according to where you live. The London not-for-profit organisation Solar for London provides free assessments and free quotes and will recommend various installers for free! Why not check to see if your government or local authority websites offer any similar schemes?

Other suggestions

1 _____ ☐

_____

2 _____ ☐

_____

3 _____ ☐

_____

4 _____ ☐

_____

5 _____ ☐

_____

	Year 1	Year 2	Year 3	Year 4	Year 5
Suggestions Score (subtotal)					

Chapter 5
Gardening – Our Direct Link with Nature

In the last two centuries, we in the West have moved from a rural to an increasingly urban society. This has led to a deep level of ignorance about how totally dependent we are on nature for our very survival. Whether it is caring for a single houseplant or a large country estate, gardening can help restore that psychological link with the cycles of nature. Gardening, however, can also have a significant nurturing or destructive effect on the environment in its own right, depending on how you go about it.

The move to chemical-based gardening has been disastrous for wildlife, as well as threatening our own health. Many ingredients in modern day herbicides, such as atrazine, lindane, hydrazine, mirex and hexachlorobenzene, are listed carcinogens (cancer-producing substances). In addition, the wholesale move to industrial agriculture since the 1950s and the planting of non-native species in gardens has led to a significant fall in habitat for many native species of insects and birds. The Woodland Trust estimates that since the 1930s, the UK has lost or damaged almost 50 per cent of what little remained of its ancient woodland. In the last century alone, nearly 50 species have become extinct in the UK. In addition, there are more than 200 species listed as being of concern on the UK Biodiversity Action Plan. Globally things are even worse. Almost a quarter of the planet's mammals face extinction according to a recent UN report, largely due to the destruction of habitat by humanity. The UN environment programme has identified more than 11,000 endangered species in total. In 2002, an area of the Amazonian rainforest the size of Belgium was razed to the ground, much of it to grow soya beans to feed Europe's livestock industry. This was a 40-per-cent increase on the previous year according to the Brazilian government. Growing some of our own food in our gardens and reducing our intake of meat will make a small contribution to reducing this international pressure on wildlife habitats.

Clinically 'immaculate' lawns have led to what the eminent Japanese environmentalist Masanobu Fukuoka refers to as 'green deserts' across our urban gardens and parks. How many animals or birds use such wide swathes of pure grass as a source of food or habitat? The answer is very few. The water used to keep these green deserts green empties rivers every summer, further threatening riverside wildlife and entailing the transport of huge amounts of water across the countryside.

My own first taste of gardening was in a top-floor flat share in Camberwell. We had a wonderful balcony the size of a small room, which was flooded with sunshine from dawn to nearly dusk. There was an elderly gay couple living next door who were avid gardeners. They were always leaning over the fence to comment on our plants, or kindly offering a cutting or some advice on how to make our balcony as horticulturally exuberant as theirs.

They gave me some spare baby tomato plants that they had raised from seed. This was my first tentative reconnection with nature and its cyclical rhythms of food production. I couldn't believe how many tomatoes my plants produced on that little inner-city roof terrace and I got real pleasure from being able to eat them. Nearly every year since, wherever I have lived, I have made sure that if I only grew one thing it would be my own tomatoes. When my then partner and I decided to buy the house I live in today, I decided it would have to have a decent garden.

I now really love my garden. It is where I replenish and restore myself after my escapades in the environmental and political fields. We had resolved not to use any artificial chemicals or fertilisers in our new garden, and so today it is completely organic. If the roses get a dose of aphids then I drench them with the water left over from washing dishes. The environmentally friendly washing-up liquid in the water is great for getting rid of them. Rather than getting loads of nasty slug and snail pellets, I simply changed the plants I grew in the garden to ones that they would not devour, such as tomatoes and blackcurrants.

Soon after moving into the cottage, I took a course in permaculture. It is an approach to life that seeks to live in harmony with nature, using what nature has provided to facilitate a more harmonious human lifestyle. It tries to use natural resources such as rainwater, solar heat and fertiliser from compostible waste to grow our own food. The idea of an edible forest has strongly influenced its thinking. It seeks to design gardens that reflect the layered structure of a forest as you move away from the house: the herbs you need daily are nearest the kitchen door, then you get the bushes, then the fruit trees and then the large trees for shelter and wood supplies.

While having only a small garden, this idea has influenced my own approach to what plants I put in my garden and where I plant them. Herbs planted near the kitchen door include thyme, sage, bay leaves and chives. I love being able to step outside the back with a small pair of scissors and harvest a batch of chives for a garnish or some fresh mint for a cup of tea. I have also managed to establish a colony of wild garlic in the tiny front garden. I dug up a few bulbs when visiting friends in Somerset, and these have very gradually started spreading across the small patch of earth in front of my house. I had not come across it before and was astonished at how this flat green leaf actually tastes deliciously of garlic. I am now able to harvest the occasional leaf for salads and love watching people's faces as they find their green salad taste garlicky!

The first thing I did in the garden after we moved in was to start planting in among the shrubs and flowers along the borders various perennial fruit-producing plants. The garden now has, with varying degrees of success, apple, pear, cherry and peach trees along with gooseberry, blackcurrant, blackberry, quince, raspberry, blueberry, hazelnut and wild strawberry bushes. The peach tree has yet to produce a blossom, never mind a peach, and the hazelnut has produced three measly hazelnuts in the ten years it has been my guest. However, all the others produce some delicious fruit which I can enjoy as I stroll around the garden. Regrettably, I have only dug a vegetable garden once or twice in the 11 years I have lived here. My life has been far too busy to nourish a regular vegetable patch.

But the garden also produces a modest but regular supply of flowers and flowering shrubs that I cut to place in vases around the house. I never buy cut flowers for the house due to the significant environmental cost involved in most commercial flower production. Thousands of tonnes of flowers are flown into Western countries every year, involving journeys of thousands of miles, simply for the flowers to be placed in a vase for a few days, and then dumped. For example, carnations from Chile are flown 7,500 miles and roses from Kenya 4,000 miles to western-European flower shops. There are no regulations about the levels of pesticide residues in imported flowers, which means that Third World workers often end up being exposed to appallingly high levels of toxic pesticides.

I attached a rain barrel to the down pipe from the kitchen lean-to roof, and this has supplied nearly all of my gardening water needs. The main problem is that the same roof is the main thoroughfare for the local cat population. They often slip on the roof tiles and crash down onto the gutter that leads to the rain barrel which disconnects it. Despite fixing it with wire, they still regularly manage to separate it!

The next task was to sort out my composting. A friend was offering labouring skills in the local green-currency scheme. I contacted him and asked if he could design a composter made out of recycled bricks. He said he could, so I collected all the waste bricks thrown away in local skips and he made a fine, big, well-aerated compost enclosure at the end of the garden that since then has taken all of my household and garden compostible waste. Twice a year I dig out the resulting compost from the access point at it's base. I distribute this home-made fertiliser to various plants around the garden that I want to feed. I also fill up three long containers in preparation for when I plant out my tomato seedlings. They do really well on this fertiliser. Tomatoes are usually the only annual plants that I find time to cultivate. (Although, from time to time, I manage basil and nasturtiums.)

Realising the problems with pesticides and having resolved not to use any in my own garden, I also began to take notice of what was happening outside my own house. I saw men spraying herbicides on our local parks and estates while dressed in moon suits. For a distance of about half of a metre above soil level, there was a strange mark on the local trees and a number of them were rotting at the point where they were being sprayed. The trees were surrounded by a semi-circle of about a square metre of soil on which nothing grew. There were similar areas along all the fencing and by the foot-paths. I found out that the local council had moved from manual to chemical weed control – all flowerbeds, bases of trees, fences and footpaths were subjected to a twice yearly drenching in chemicals.

Since the first generation of the pesticides, each wave has been sold to the public as being 'safe' for human health only to be subsequently found to be damaging to the lungs, nervous or immune systems or indeed to be carcinogenic. The latest is atrazine, which is now being banned by the European Union.

In addition to these dangers to humans, they harm our precious environment, including beneficial organisms such as honeybees and birds, and increasingly threaten the purity of our underground aquifers. In the United States, at least one and more often several pesticides are found in over 90 per cent of fish and stream-water samples. £2 billion worth of capital investment in water-treatment facilities has had to be invested in the United Kingdom alone between 1990 and 2000, to remove pesticides from water in order to make it safe for drinking. And the maintenance cost of these facilities is over £100 million a year. It is the general public who has to pay for cleaning up this pollution in either taxes or higher water charges, as the cost is not included in the retail price of the pesticides.

Along with some friends, I started campaigning for a return to manual weeding locally. If I would not tolerate chemicals being sprayed on my own garden, why should I be happy with them on my local streets and parks? Following a short but positive campaign, we were delighted when the local council agreed that as each contract for grounds maintenance on parks, council housing estates and streets came up for renewal, the tender would be based on the return to manual removal of weeds. At the modest cost of approximately an extra £70,000 (US$127,000 or 100,000) a year to the annual budget, the council became one of the first in the country to start phasing out its pesticide use. This works out at about half a penny a week for each resident in the borough. I think that is a pretty cheap price to pay to protect our children and our environment from further exposure to toxic chemicals. It just shows that it really is possible for one person to raise an environmental issue and create genuine change in their local community by working with their friends.

My next gardening adventure outside my home was to ensure my local public green open space, Burgess Park, was protected and enhanced. Why shouldn't my neighbours in the nearby tower blocks also enjoy the nourishment from nature that I enjoyed in my garden? When I first got involved the local council hadn't done any tree planting for years. They hadn't made up their minds what the final design of the park would be and total paralysis had set in. I spoke to one council officer who had been planning a community tree planting for over four years, but couldn't decide where to do it because of uncertainties. I heard that they were planning to tarmac over a large area to use as a car park. This acted as the stimulus for my first major direct action.

I revived the local park action group and contacted the local Friends of the Earth and Wildlife Trust groups. I suggested a community planting, and three weeks later we had over 50 people on a Sunday morning planting hundreds of little saplings on the land where the tarmac had been planned.

We had been told that none of the trees would survive, as the local kids would destroy them. Ignoring this advice instead, we asked the kids to join in planting the trees. This gave them a feeling of ownership over them and only about ten per cent were pulled up in the following weeks. A couple of volunteers and I simply returned every week for a month and replanted the few that had been messed with.

It was very rewarding when, within a few months of the saplings being planted, I could already spy small songbirds alighting on the frail young branches. That was over ten years ago, and there is now a wonderful horseshoe of tall trees. Whenever I need to boost my belief that it is possible to achieve positive change, I take a walk to this little piece of woodland and it recharges my soul. Many of the trees are already over ten metres tall, replacing a derelict and neglected area of urban blight with a beautiful green landscape.

I then got involved with saving the park as a whole (see Chapter 10) – and I also became the open spaces coordinator for my local Friends of the Earth group. Through this role, I worked with other nearby groups whose sites were at risk, and through these people I began to hear about the threats across the country to numerous local open spaces. For tens of thousands of people in just my community, these open spaces are the closest thing they have to a garden – to the natural world. From the beautiful ancient temperate forests in Canada and the west coast of America to the lush rich tropical forests of Indonesia and Brazil, our wasteful consumerist utilitarianism that seeks to destroy these ancient forests also seeks to build on our children's playgrounds and our local nature reserves. It is a wastefulness that can be successfully tackled and reversed, which is what this book is all about.

Ensure your own gardening is as environmentally sustainable as possible in your circumstances. Your actions, no matter how small initially, can spread out in waves and positively affect thousands of others. Whether it is a simple window box, a nice big balcony or a full blown garden, there is always something you can do to move things forward. The list below should help plant a few ideas to help you get started today.

How to score

3   if you do the suggestion nearly all the time

2   if you do it occasionally or fairly often

1   if you hardly ever do it

0   if you never do it

Suggestions that save you money

205 Use the compost from your own compost heap rather than artificial fertilisers. ☐

This saves you from spending money on potting compost.

206 Switch to organic gardening methods, which do not use chemical weed-killers or artificial fertilisers. ☐

I have not spent a single penny on fertilisers, pesticides or herbicides in my garden over the last ten years. Despite this, strange as it may seem, it is still wonderfully green and productive. I prefer to spend the money on fruit trees and shrubs instead.

207 Don't buy peat moss as a garden fertiliser or for your potting plants. ☐

It may be natural, but peat moss is produced from precious yet fast-disappearing wetland wildlife habitats. There are plenty of other organic alternatives on the market to choose from, in addition to creating your own from your household/garden compost. Bought peat-free compost is almost exactly the same price as the habitat-destructive peat moss.

208 Use natural organic fertiliser in your garden made from comfrey leaves. ☐

Comfrey leaves are rich in potash and nitrogen. Simply plant a patch in a corner of your garden and you will be able to harvest its leaves twice a year by cutting it back to a hands-breadth above the soil. Ensure you plant it in the right place first time, as it is very hard to get rid of once planted. To use as a fertiliser simply dig it into the soil, use it as a mulch on top or soak in water in a covered container and use it as a liquid fertiliser. Once you've paid for the initial seeds, all future fertiliser coming from the patch will be free!

209 Include plants such a legumes that actually restore ☐

the nitrogen to the soil they are growing in. Legume species include clover, beans, lentils and alfalfa.

Most other plants consume nitrogen from the soil; growing legumes will reduce your need to add artificial fertilisers, most of which are nitrogen based.

210 Reserve an area in your garden for nettles.

Nettles provide wonderful food for many caterpillars before they turn into butterflies. Remember, nettles also add nitrogen to your soil and young nettles are delicious boiled like spinach with butter and salt added for flavour. You will not be stung if you use gloves when picking them. Cut them back at midsummer, and throw them on the compost heap where they act as an activator. Spinach costs the equivalent of two packets of crisps per bunch at the supermarket, so using young boiled nettles saves this expense.

211 You can use the leaves from the tomato plants, nasturtiums and indeed from any dandelions growing wild in your garden, to add flavour to your salads.

Plastic bags of mixed salad leaves can cost the equivalent of four packets of crisps in the supermarkets.

212 Allow annual and perennial plants to self-seed in your garden.

It means that you will not have to go out and buy seeds or potted versions next spring.

213 Enjoy a less-than 'perfectly weed-free' lawn.

Using loads of herbicides to maintain a perfect lawn is toxic to the wildlife you want to encourage. You might even come to enjoy a wider variety of plants and even get to love daisies. It also reduces stress levels associated with the irrational fear of weeds appearing in the grass.

214 Throw your used dishwater on any plants that are infested with aphids (greenfly).

Environmentally-friendly washing-up liquid is amazingly effective against aphids. So you can have beautiful roses without nasty pesticides, which saves about the price of a reasonable bottle of wine per litre.

215 If you are tolerably fit, when buying a new lawn-mower buy a hand-pushed model. (Not recommended if your garden is huge!)

A traditional, lightweight mechanical lawnmower costs about the price of a good quality pair of jeans. It obviously uses zero watts of electricity and helps keep you fit. An electrical lawnmower, however, can cost about the price of nearly four pairs of jeans, uses 1,100 watts of electricity per hour and doesn't make you slim and beautiful!

216 If you have a small garden, avoid buying an electric hedge-trimmer.

Again the exercise will help keep you trim rather than feeding global warming! An electric hedge-trimmer can cost around the price of two good pairs of jeans and uses 500 watts of electricity per hour.

217 If you need new garden furniture, first see if you can get it second-hand, or if not, consider buying garden furniture from recycled plastic or wood.

Buying second-hand means you know you are definitely not buying wood from ancient tropical or temperate forests.

218 If building a new path or flowerbed, try to use reused bricks and paving slabs.

This reduces the clay resources locked up in bricks and eliminates the energy used to fire new bricks. I found enough bricks

97

in skips to build a new permanent compost heap in my garden. Don't forget to ask permission before raiding a skip! Allow gaps between the bricks or slabs to allow the rain to soak into the garden rather than straight into storm drains. As well as watering your garden, it helps to avoid flash flooding.

Suggestions that cost nothing

219   Plant at least one tree annually to compensate for your CO_2 emissions. If you don't have enough space yourself, find a local park, wildlife site or woodland that could benefit from another tree and ask permission to plant one there.

Some wildlife trusts have free native-tree schemes, whereby they give free saplings to members of the public to plant. Alternatively, you could grow your own for free from seeds – such as acorns – which can add to the satisfaction.

220   Get permission to replant relevant seedlings that pop up in your garden in a local park, once they are mature enough to survive independently.

These trees by locking up CO_2 will help compensate for your own CO_2 emissions.

221   Plant native species that encourage wildlife.

Native trees and plants usually provide food for a greater range of insects, birds and animals than imported species. In the UK, the Linnean Society has an online database at the National History Museum website www.nhm.ac.uk, where you can type in your postcode and it will come up with the species native to your locality. In the US, The Lady Bird Johnson Wildflower Center's website www.wildflower.org has a database where, if you fill in the state you live in, it will provide a list of native plants for your state.

222   Do not remove the remains of perennial plants until winter is over.

Their seeds provide precious food for wildlife.

223 Provide homes for insects by leaving some leaf piles undisturbed, placing old timber or logs in a shady area, or leaving bundles of twigs in a corner where they will be left alone.

Insects provide food for birds and small mammals such as hedgehogs, voles and shrews, as well as being interesting in themselves as wildlife.

224 If you have a pile of old rubble lying around, instead of going to the trouble of removing it, throw some soil from your compost heap on it and turn it into a beautiful rockery.

This will cut down on heavy waste and create an interesting corner for your garden.

225 Choose plants that require low amounts of water when planting fresh stock.

Lavender, thyme, red-hot pokers, rosemary, sage, poppies and cornflowers are some examples that will do well in an English garden. Ask your local garden centre for more recommendations or recommendations that will suit the climate in which your garden is situated.

226 If you know where there is a large amount of wild garlic, carefully take a couple of bulbs for your garden. Alternatively, if you catch them when seeding, take the seeds instead. But do not do this with rare or legally protected wild plants!

Its soft, wide green leaves taste deliciously like garlic-flavoured spinach and can be used raw in salads or cooked like spinach. The flowers and bulbs can also be eaten, but have a stronger taste of garlic.

227 When laying new lawns, ensure you choose a drought-tolerant seed mix.

This will reduce future watering needs for your garden.

228 If you have a reasonable-sized lawn, consider cutting it to different heights and planting an area of it with wild-flower meadow seeds.

This will enable it to provide food for a greater variety of local birds and insects.

229 Find out if your local authority has a chipping service for chopped branches. If they don't, ask them why not!

Many councils provide a tree-chipping service to residents. Their machines chop up the large tree branches into small chips which you can use in your garden as mulch or compost. Sometimes these are free or they make only a small charge. If your council doesn't provide such a service, there may be commercial contractors in your neighbourhood who do so. Chipping your tree waste reduces the waste stream and ensures that precious nutrients locked up in the wood are not lost to the garden. Many councils provide free tree-chipping services especially for discarded Christmas trees: check their websites for details.

230 Instead of buying a traditional dead sawn-off or plastic Christmas tree for your home or office, buy a live young native evergreen tree, such as a holly tree in a pot, and decorate it instead. Then, when you are finished with it, you can plant it in your garden or in a local wildlife site or park.

This cuts down on waste and on the petro-chemicals used to produce artificial Christmas trees, as well of course of adding to your local stock of trees, which absorb CO_2.

231   Look after your local street trees. Normally they don't need watering, but they may need some in drought periods in summer during their early years.

If they are suffering, the leaves will wilt or a significant number will go brown. Give them a good drenching with a couple of buckets of water every couple of weeks during the drought. Local authorities don't usually have the means to ensure this happens in such emergencies. A good drenching ensures that the water penetrates deeply, thereby not encouraging shallow roots and ensuring it survives the drought. I had to do this with a four-year-old street tree planted across from my house last summer. A couple of buckets of water three times during the drought ensured its revival. I now have a fond affinity for it, feeling that I helped save its life.

232   If you do not have any street trees on the road where you live, contact your local authority to see if they will plant some.

The leaves on street trees can reduce street dust pollution by up to 90 per cent. I made a phone call to my local council last spring suggesting that they plant some trees on a bleak street near my home. Six months later I came home to find the street lined with six new trees planted along it's length. The smallest things in life can give you the nicest feelings!

233   If you live in rented or communal accommodation, see if you can persuade your landlord to install a community composting facility if there is any small area of soil on your property. If this is not possible, see if there are any allotments in your neighbourhood that might be willing to take your own organic waste.

Some local authorities have community composting schemes. Check their website or call them to find out. Composting reduces the amount of needless rubbish going to landfills.

234 When out and about and you are eating fruit, drop the banana skin or apple core in a plant pot or hedgerow instead of in a municipal bin.

It will break down quickly and naturally and help enrich the soil.

235 If you are a member of a golf club, ask if they've adopted a greener golf course policy. If not, propose they adopt one at your next AGM.

Both in the US and Europe there is an increasing awareness of the high environmental costs of golf courses, which range from the destruction of natural habitats, use of pesticides, artificial fertilisers and huge water consumption. These can be ameliorated in many ways if the commitment is there. Information on how to do this is available from the European Golf Association's Ecology Unit and the US Golf Association.

236 Implement the concepts of permaculture in your garden's layout.

In his book The One-Straw Revolution, *Masanobu Fukuoka describes permaculture as a philosophy of working with rather than against nature; of protracted and thoughtful observation rather than protracted and thoughtless labour. It looks at plants and animals in all their functions rather than treating any area as a single-product system.*

Suggestions that cost a small amount extra

237 Try to have a range of plants that flower at different stages of the year to ensure there is always plenty of nectar available from the flowers for passing butterflies and other insects.

The Henry Doubleday Research Association (HDRA) in the UK has special packets of wildflower seeds available for the price of a half litre of wine. The Lady Bird Johnson Wildflower

Center has a database of native plant suppliers for across the US on its website www.wildflower.org.

238 Suggested favourites in the UK for bees include primrose, bluebells, foxgloves, nasturtiums and gorse. Some of these such as primrose and nasturtiums can be grown on balconies or in window boxes even if you haven't got a garden. Everyone can help provide for our little natural neighbours!

The HDRA also has special packets of wildflower seeds that are specially designed to feed bumble-bees similarly at the price of about a half litre of wine. Of course, bumble-bees will return the favour by helping to pollinate your own flowers!

239 Green your walls! This can be done with a variety of climbing plants. Ivy is good for north-facing walls and is a treasure trove for a whole host of insects and birds, but don't use it on house walls as it can cause damage to the mortar. Try a grapevine on a south facing wall and the fruit will be popular with your local little neighbours such as birds and moths. If you want the reward of a beautiful smell, try some sweet-smelling jasmine on west facing walls or, for a rich source of nectar, plant wisteria against south-facing walls. Again, a garden is not necessary for you to help – ivy can grow almost anywhere, so try some from your window box.

These can all provide a habitat and source of food for a whole host of birds and insects.

240 Use slug and snail traps that avoid the use of chemical pesticides – many use beer as bait, as slugs crave yeast.

Slug traps, which can contain hundreds of dead slugs, cost about the price of a good bottle of wine and all you have to do is empty it into the compost heap when full. (You do not have *to touch a single slug!) Personally, I decided only to grow plants in my garden that slugs won't devour. This means I now look on them as friends who help with my composting.*

241 Investigate biological pest control products, which use naturally occurring microbes that can be bought to control pests in your garden if necessary.

It costs about the same as two bottles of wine to treat a 40-square-metre garden.

242 Avoid buying cut flowers – buy home-grown non-peat-reared flowering plants instead. Or better still, grow your own flowers. Bulbs are great because they pop up year after year without you having to do any work. Flowering shrubs are good too as their cut, blossom-laden branches can provide wonderful colour for your home without requiring much work.

The cut flower industry is often a source of very heavy herbicide use due to the vast unnatural monoculture of single flower varieties. This causes severe health problems for many workers in the industry. Much of these flowers are flown in from great distances causing heavy transport emissions. Producing your own flowers saves you money too, as bunches of flowers can vary in cost from a pint of beer to four or five bottles of wine.

243 If you have a large garden or live in the countryside, plant native evergreen trees to protect your home from the winter's prevailing winds.

This helps reduce heat loss from your home in winter.

244 If you are having your garden professionally land-scaped, try and employ a landscape gardener who specialises in environmentally responsible gardening design.

Incorporating such measures into the design means that the benefits will be felt for the lifetime of the garden and will affect the amount of watering and nourishment the garden will require and the amount of wildlife it will support.

245 Create a wildlife section in your garden where you allow wild plants to flourish.

This will seed itself and cost nothing, or you can buy starter packets of organic wildlife seeds for about the price of a half litre of wine. There are even ranges of wild plants whose green leaves and shoots are edible.

246 If you haven't got one already, create a pond to attract and support more wildlife. Insects, frogs and birds will love it. If you can't create a pond, at least always leave a container with some water in or buy/create a birdbath.

Ensure there is at least one side of the pond that is gently sloped to allow creatures like hedgehogs that fall in by accident an escape route! Regularly refresh water in a container in freezing weather to ensure some drinkable water is available. Place it where cats can't hide within easy striking distance.

247 Mix in various food-producing plants in your ornamental borders such as blackcurrant, gooseberry, quince, blackberries, loganberries, blueberries etc.

248 Plant culinary herbs in your rockeries or in pots near your kitchen door for easy access when cooking. Basil is not only delicious but is quite pretty as a window-ledge plant – a very common sight in Greece.

Herbs are quite easy to grow from seed, but can be bought from your local garden centre for the price of about two packets of crisps per plant. Once established, perennial herbs such as chives, thyme, rosemary and sage will provide you with plenty of fresh culinary herbs for your kitchen for years, repaying the initial small investment over and over. Being able to pluck fresh basil leaves from my windowsill whenever I need some, is one of my small pleasures in life!

249 If you have only a small garden, you can buy fruit trees with specially designed dwarf roots that ensure that the tree does not grow too big – these include pear, apple, plum etc.

Growing your own fruit reduces the need for transporting fruit half-way round the world just for you to eat.

250 Grow your own tomato plants from seed. There is nothing like the pleasure of picking a juicy ripe tomato from your own vine, bursting it with your teeth and allowing the juice to fill your mouth on a summer's day! Grow the tomatoes in compost from your own garden to truly close the environmental loop.

A packet of organic tomato seeds costs only around the price of four packets of crisps. Organic gro-bags cost about the price of a good bottle of wine each. As well as saving the money, you also save on the unnecessary transport and wasting the heavy plastic bags when the tomatoes are finished if you use your own compost.

251 Ensure that your garden's security lights are triggered by sensors rather than being left on all night.

Sensor lights cost about the price of a pair of jeans upwards, but will save you electricity from burning unnecessarily all night long, all year round, if security is an issue in your home.

252 If you have a large area of grass in your garden, consider replacing some of it with more productive plants.

Switching grassy areas to shrubs or fruit and vegetables will add richness to the amount of wildlife your garden can support or the amount of delicious home-grown food your garden gives you as a gift back from nature. Alternatively, there are a number of attractive ground-covering plants that you can use instead and that avoid the need to be watered and cut so often. Ask your local garden centre for species that are suitable for where you live.

253 Put up bat boxes. Bats eat thousands of mosquitoes in a night! Ideally place it on the southeast side of a house or tree, at least three metres up. Don't disturb them during hibernation and don't use wood that is treated with preservatives or paint – both of which can kill them.

As well as helping your wildlife, you could also be reducing your local blood-sucking mosquito population! With climate change, the population of mosquitoes is rising in the UK but we are wiping out the habitats for our native bats. Batty wouldn't you say? An Forest Stewardship Council (FSC) certified wood bat box from the Royal Society for the Protection of Birds (RSPB) costs about the price of a couple of bottles of wine. In North America you can buy bat boxes online from Bat Conservation International at www.batcon.org.

254 Place bird nesting boxes in appropriate places. Ensure that you clean them out after each season as they can collect mites and fleas that may infect the next year's nestlings.

This will counteract our massive loss in natural habitats, but don't place them in the path of the prevailing wind or in sunny spots. Four boxes is probably the maximum a small garden can take. Make sure that they are different sizes. Many birds are territorial with their own kind and will fight to protect their space, but will live amicably with other species. Wooden bird boxes cost the equivalent of between two and four bottles of wine.

255 If you have cold winters that kill off vulnerable native birds, buy a bird feeder.

This will help them survive when food is scarce. This can help make up for the millions of birds killed each year by our population explosion in domestic cats.

256   Place bird tables or feeders high off the ground – plant holly or other prickly plant underneath.

This prevents cats from climbing up and devouring your visiting bird life! Never place birdfeed on the ground where they are most vulnerable from cat attacks. In winter, birds can lose up to a third of their body weight just keeping themselves warm, and so emergency food can be really welcome at this time. A word of warning: do not feed birds salted peanuts or other salted food, as salt is often poisonous to birds. (This does not apply to sea birds, who have become especially adapted to cope with salt!)

257   If you can't do without a cat or dog, neuter them.

Don't let them contribute to even greater overpopulation. Neutering can cost up to the price of three pairs of jeans, but many animal charities operate free or cheap neutering schemes. Check the web or phone to see if your local animal charity or authority operates such a scheme.

258   If you have a cat, buy it a collar with a bell on it.

This will help warn birds that it is about and so save many lives in return for a tiny investment.

259   If you have access to a garden or even a small area of soil, you can install a composter. The latest generation can take even animal or dairy products, as they are rodent proof.

A basic composter from one of the big hardware companies costs only the equivalent of one pair of jeans. You can make your own with timber rescued from a skip. Wooden compost heaps are extremely simple in design and almost anyone with a hammer and saw can make one. It is really only a four-sided square box with a space at the bottom to dig out the rich new compost. Composters that can take animal products are usually only available by mail order and are a bit more expensive. You could even compost using the old-fashioned hole in the ground, which obviously costs nothing, but do not put animal or dairy products in this as it will attract vermin and make you rather unpopular with your neighbours!

260 Choose wood chippings, gravel or wooden decking (FSC international standard or recycled wood of course!) for any new paths if you cannot get any recycled bricks or paving stones.

This allows the rain to soak into your garden rather than into a storm drain.

Suggestions that require a significant capital investment

261 If installing new security lamps in your garden or outside your front door, consider installing solar-powered lights.

A top quality set of two solar-powered lamps plus people sensors costs about the same as an economy fridge.

262 If you are replacing fencing, consider using a living fence – ie a hedge. Avoid the single species hedges so common in many gardens; plant a whole variety of native hedging varieties instead.

Hedge plants can be bought for as little as the equivalent of a half bottle of wine depending on the variety. Regular wooden fencing costs from about the equivalent of two bottles of wine per two-metre section upwards. As well as saving resources, your hedge will provide a habitat and food source for many local species, increasing the number of birds that will visit your garden.

263 If a hedge is not appropriate for replacing your old fencing, investigate the range of recycled plastic fencing now available.

This is available from about the equivalent of three bottles of wine per metre.

Other suggestions

1 _____

2 _____

3 _____

4 _____

5 _____

_____

	Year 1	Year 2	Year 3	Year 4	Year 5
Suggestions Score (subtotal)					

Chapter 6
Real Food or Chemical Food?

Nearly every celebration or party involves the consumption of food and drink. It provides the raw material for the maintenance and repair of our bodies and is the source of the energy that enables us to operate and move. But where our food is grown, how it is grown, packaged, transported, cooked and its waste disposed of, are all questions that not only have profound environmental consequences but can also affect our own health.

Many people give no thought to where or how the food on their table comes from, other than that it comes in nice attractive packaging from the supermarket. The average family meal travels tens of thousands of miles. We consume without a second thought apples from New Zealand, green beans from Kenya, tomatoes from Crete, beef from Argentina and so on. This would be unheard of in previous generations. While the growth of international trade can lead to greater international communication and understanding, the current massive explosion in the distances food travels is having a disastrous effect on our environment with road and air transport being one of the fastest growing sources of global warming emissions. (Transporting food by plane uses 40 times the energy as transporting it by sea.)

One of the most farcical aspects of this trade is that often countries are exporting the same products to each other. For example, the UK exports millions of litres of yoghurt each year to Germany, but Germany also exports millions of litres of its yoghurt to the UK! This happens between many EU countries – we have all these lorries transporting yoghurt back and forth absolutely pointlessly and the environment continues to suffer. There is no point in having a wonderfully successful market economy if it destroys the ability of the planet's environment to support itself. So until we devise systems of transport that are environmentally benign, it makes more sense to source our food closer to home.

Taking food for granted in the West may not be a possibility for the next generation if climate change continues. In the first four years of our new century the planet consumed more grain than it produced, reducing world grain reserves to their lowest point since records began in the 1960s. The unprecedented heat wave that hit Europe in the summer of 2003 devastated the grain crops, with yields being reduced by as much as 75 per cent in many countries. Large sections of South Africa have had their lowest recorded rainfall since records began, with severe drought causing crop failures across neighbouring southern African states, causing the price of basic foodstuffs to rise. Large swathes of the Midwestern United States also suffered severe drought throughout 2003. It doesn't take much imagination to see the potential cataclysmic consequences for food production if scientists are right about global weather patterns changing even further. With the world's human population now inexorably rising above 6 billion people, the risks of widespread famine will be immense.

Globalisation has led to the domination of monocultural food production. This form of crop production involves the handing over of farmland to vast swathes of the same crop which are then planted year after year, allowing extreme specialisation. The abandoning of crop rotation and the traditional mix of crops has meant that synthetic fertiliser requirements have risen inexorably. Large-scale agriculture carries a far higher risk of plant disease and pest infestation than traditional mixed farming, and so uses more pesticides and herbicides. Many traditional habitats are being ploughed up or doused with a chemical cocktail, bringing a tragic reduction in the range of wildlife the countryside supports. Monocultural production results in millions of tonnes of topsoil being lost annually from our fields. The US government calculates that six metric tonnes of topsoil is being lost annually per acre from land farmed with industrial processes. The state of California estimates that 2.5 cm (0.98 inches) of topsoil is being lost every year from such farmland. As it takes up to 500 years for nature to create 2.5 cm of topsoil, this means that the soil is being lost at a rate over 20-times faster than it is being replaced. Agriculture's chemical dependency has provided only a temporary mirage of plentiful cheap food. Industrially produced food is a severe threat to the ability of future generations to live off the land. Can we really say to our grandchildren that our temporary 'cheap' industrial food was worth squandering their soil inheritance?

Not content with making farming chemically addicted, the big industrial agro-chemical seed companies have combined with the pharmaceutical industry to genetically modify both plants and animals. Many of the claims made for GM foods have one by one been demolished over recent years. They claimed that during crop trials, neighbouring crops would not be contaminated. This was extraordinary in the light of the fact that any 12-year-old child knows that pollen can be carried many miles not only by the wind but also by bees and other insects. Indeed, farmers in Canada have been successfully sued by the huge international GM conglomerates for using the seed from their own crops, after they had been contaminated with pollen from neighbouring GM crops. As a result, many Canadian farmers are now afraid of planting the seeds from their own crops, as they did for generations, as they cannot be sure it is safe from GM pollen. George Orwell never predicted that it would come to this in his book *1984*.

They claimed that 'super weeds' would not result from planting GM crops that were resistant to a number of different weed killers. In the jargon this is called 'gene-stacking' – the weeds would grab the pesticide and herbicide resistant genes from each subsequent GM plant that it encountered. However, such 'impossible' super weeds have already emerged in Canada within a few short years of widespread GM crop planting there.

They claimed that the new GM crops would reduce the amount of pesticide being used, yet in most of the American states where GM crops have been planted this has not been the case, and so it goes on.

The former UK environment minister, Michael Meacher, has stated that there have been hardly any safety studies done on the consequences for human health of GM foods. Of the few that have been carried out, some have shown the ability of some genetically modified genes to cross into the DNA of bacteria lining the human gut.

Accompanying the increasing industrialisation of crop production has been the industrialisation of food processing. As food companies grew, so did the necessity of adding various chemicals to assist preservation and enhance the taste, smell and colour of food. Now, the list of ingredients on many supermarket food products more often resemble a chemistry lesson than something found in nature. The huge buying power of such a small number of supermarket chains has also had disastrous effects. They only buy a few varieties of vegetable and fruit, which will fit with the specific requirements of such large operations. Hundreds of precious fruit and vegetable varieties are being lost due to this short-sightedness. As well as being a sad loss in it's own right, this is dangerous to future food security, as it leaves less varieties in reserve, in case a new disease wipes out the few varieties now actually being massplanted.

At the same time, the perceived need to brand food to increase sales of one particular company over another has led to an explosion in the amount of packaging food is subjected to. It is easy to think that this has always been the case, but it has only been in the last few decades that the phenomenon of huge, overflowing, domestic rubbish bins has emerged. Many items, which now have sophisticated packaging had very little or no packaging in former times. I still remember as a very small child playing with the small enamel bucket in which the milk was collected from the local dairy in the small Irish town of Thurles, County Tipperary where I was born. Potatoes came in a large brown paper sack, which was thrown on the compost heap when it was empty. No waste emerged from the use of either product, not even an aluminium bottle top.

When I returned from the Amazon, I slowly started to change my food-buying habits. I had already become a vegetarian by accident when I shared a flat with a friend whose disgust at the sight of meat was subtly catching. It was only later that I learnt all the environmental and cruelty arguments for vegetarianism. I had no idea for example that over 51 billion animals are slaughtered for human consumption worldwide every year according to the UN Food and Agriculture Organisation. That includes over 200 million in the UK and over 10 billion in the US every year. The cruelty involved in the production of many animal products shames us all. Take for example *pâté de foie gras*, where corn is forcibly fed down the throat of the poor geese to ensure that their liver expands. Or veal, where calves are penned in tiny spaces so that they have no opportunity to use their muscles so they stay white and tender. Not to mention the cruelty represented by the intensive farming of more everyday meat from chickens, turkeys, cows and pigs.

The massive human population explosion over the last century has put a huge pressure on the planet's resources. The world's population in 1900 was only 1.6 billion. By 2003, it had mushroomed to 6.3 billion people. Millions of acres of wilderness and rainforest are still being cleared for agriculture. Increasing wealth in the West has led to a huge increase in meat consumption. It takes much more land to produce one pound of beef protein than it does to produce a pound of vegetable protein, such as that contained in nuts or rice. It is estimated that one acre of land produces 30,000 lb (13,500 kg) of carrots but only 250 lb (112.5 kg) of beef. Over 50 per cent of the UK cereal crop and over one third of the total world cereal crop is used to feed animals, and 80 per cent of UK and 70 per cent of world agricultural land is used for livestock rearing. According to the Vegetarian Society, over 150 billion litres (39 billion US gallons) of water are used in the UK alone simply for meat production. It takes 900 litres (234 US gallons) to produce one kilogram of wheat, while it takes an astonishing 50-100,000 litres (13–26,000 US gallons) to produce one kilogram of meat. Fifteen per cent of the world-wide emissions of the powerful global warming gas methane comes from farm animals.

It is now estimated that more than one third of the earth's total landmass is taken up with livestock rearing. I can't see how this is justifiable in a world where hundreds of millions of people suffer from hunger and starvation. More and more land in the Third World is being cleared in order to provide the feed for the cattle we consume in the West, rather than food for the people who actually live in those countries. The diversion of grain supplies into animal feed of course means that the remaining grain becomes more expensive for the world's poor who depend on it for survival.

The Yanomami, with whom I stayed while in the Amazon, generally had meat and fish around once a week. While not being vegetarian they did not over-consume their natural resources. I remember on the first morning I woke up in the shabono (village compound), one of the families I was staying with took me on a trek to find the animal that had been killed the day before by one of the hunters. After the kill, the hunter had left the carcass and returned to the village to tell the others where it was. I followed my hosts through the forest to the place indicated. There lay a dead orang-utan. The family quickly got to work, and it was skinned and loaded up within half an hour before we returned to the village. The meat was cooked that evening, but the hunter wasn't allowed to partake. Thus their culture had developed a system where greed could not kick in and destroy the very source in nature of their animal protein. It is a pity we don't have a system that prevents us overindulging our taste for meat too! Human beings really don't need to eat meat every day of the week. Not only is it unnecessary but over-consumption of meat leads to many diseases including obesity, heart disease and increased prevalence of certain cancers.

It is estimated that over half a million porpoises and dolphins die each year in the drift-nets of our huge industrial factory ships. The Yanomami, however, had also developed a method of fishing that prevented such destruction, but provided them with their needs. Early one morning a small group of men from the shabono and I took canoes upriver. We stopped at the side of the forest and went in a little way. There they pulped the leaves of a particular bush using large poles. I was given a pole to help with the mashing, but despite being a fit dancer at the time, I was soon sweating and exhausted while those around me showed no sign of strain. We then took the resulting mash back to the shabono and the entire village then came with us to the banks of another small river. They all came laden with baskets. The men spread the mash in the water and then I realised what the whole mysterious operation had been about. Within a few minutes small and medium-sized fish floated unconscious up to the surface. The people started gathering what they wanted into the baskets that they had brought with them. I was initially concerned about the wholesale destruction apparently wrought by the poisonous mash. But after half an hour's harvesting, I saw that the fish that were unwanted began to recover and swam off. The mash had only stunned them so some could be harvested. I was struck by the positive contrast to the destructiveness of the so-called 'civilised' West's huge fishing fleets. The UN Food and Agriculture Organisation calculate that 57 billion pounds of sea life is caught and wasted every year, as trawlers catch and kill a whole variety of organisms for which they have no use.

Our civilisation is devouring the world's fish at an alarming rate. The teeming cod fisheries off the coast of Newfoundland have almost totally gone. The herring and mackerel fisheries off the south-west coast of Ireland have been devastated and the North Sea fisheries have declined to such an extent that scientists fear for its very future if drastic measures are not taken, as have the fisheries in the Sea of Cortez in California. More than five per cent of the dolphin population off the coast of France is killed every year, which is three times faster than they can be replaced. Worldwide, large fish populations have dropped by over 90 per cent over the last 50 years. The UN estimates that over three quarters of worldwide commercial fisheries have been fully exploited. Yet the Yanomami have lived in one section of the Amazon basin for well over 20,000 years and still their environment produces meat and fish for them as it has for millennia. If only we could say the same for our own lifestyles.

Worrying about the environmental consequences of my meat and fish consumption was one of the few areas of my life that I did not have to reassess after returning from my stay with the Yanomami. It was already something I avoided, so didn't have to worry about how much I ate, whether it was produced organically or whether any cruelty was involved in its production. But up till then I hadn't given any thought to the food I actually did eat. I did 100 per cent of my shopping at the local supermarket and paid no attention to anything except price and whether I fancied it.

As I was a freelance ballet dancer at the time, I was on a tight budget and organic food at that time was significantly more expensive than factory-farmed food, so I resolved to buy one organic product each time I did a shop at the supermarket. I remember organic tomato ketchup was one of my first purchases and I also remember being stunned by reading the list of ingredients. Not only had they all been grown without the use of chemical fertiliser or herbicides, but there was no added sugar, no added artificial preservatives, no artificial colours or flavours and yet it still tasted delicious and lasted just as long in my cupboard.

From this first step, my shopping and food consumption underwent a slow and gentle revolution. I started to find other sources of organic products in my area. There were two health-food shops on my way home from town that stocked organic products unavailable in the supermarket. I then discovered a food co-operative that was run by volunteers committed to local people on low incomes having access to healthy organic foods. It was a dream shop for me. It not only stocked a large range of organic foods, but it also had a policy of avoiding unnecessary packaging. Organic rice and muesli, for example, were kept in huge bins and you brought your own bags to fill up. So cardboard boxes, plastic wrapping and foil bags became a thing of the past when buying these products, as they did for my chickpeas, herbal teas, fruit and vegetables. It is awful to see that some supermarkets have now taken packaging to its ultimate level of nonsense; with hard plastic containers for each individual pear and apple, and a label on them identifying them as an apple or a pear!

A couple of years after I returned from the Amazon, a community co-operative was set up locally to deal with our community's environmental sustainability issues. It was called Green Adventures. They were full of exciting ideas such as initiating community orchards and gardens to produce healthy organic food for local consumption. One of their more successful initiatives – the Green Ventures Box Scheme, in which organic fruit and veg is delivered by bicycles with trailers attached – is still going to this day. Deliverers were paid in the local green currency, 'Pecks', and many of them used their Pecks to purchase food from the scheme. Some time later they expanded the range of produce to include organic bread and free-range eggs. They sought to reduce the waste mountain by selecting produce that had a minimum of packaging, and delivering in reused plastic bags supplied to them by their customers.

As soon as I heard about the scheme, I joined up. I was not only delighted to be able to support a project that was so positive, but I was also able to pay for my deliveries in Pecks as I was a member of the local green-currency scheme. Of course, the idea of not having to go out shopping and lug home my weekly load of fruit and vegetables was also attractive! The selection of fruit and vegetables you receive is decided by the scheme, according to what is in season. I quite like the weekly surprise of seeing what vegetables are in season each week.

I only realised how far removed many people had become from the sources of their food when staying with some friends. Their house had a row of apple trees at the end of the garden which were becoming laden with a bumper crop of apples. One Saturday morning one of my friends arrived home with a load of shopping which included a number of plastic-wrapped containers of apples. Surprised, I asked why she was buying apples when she had loads of her own, just waiting to be picked from the tree. The answer came back that it was easier to go and buy them in the supermarket. It is this removal from the reality of where and how food is produced that is contributing to the increasing destructiveness of our food supply.

During the time I took off work to focus on my political campaigns, I signed up with the box scheme as a deliverer and used my Pecks to purchase a weekly supply of fruit and vegetables. This helped eke out the small bequest I had from my mother and enabled me to survive the duration of the campaign. I ended up doing a number of TV, radio and newspaper interviews – the image of a political activist delivering organic supplies with a cycle trailer was a temptation many of the media interviewers could not resist. I was then able to promote cycling and organic box schemes to millions of people without even having to try!

I continued my weekly delivery round for nearly four years after returning to work, reverting to paying for deliveries as I became too busy. Through this box scheme, the co-operative shop and a couple of local health-food shops as well as the occasional foray to a farmer's market, I am now almost 100-per-cent free of supermarkets for my shopping. The sudden upsurge in farmers markets, where the producers of good-quality food manage to cut out the middlemen and supermarket giants and sell their produce direct to the consumer, has been a wonderfully positive sign. I find nearly the only time I now supermarket shop is when I'm having friends over to dinner and want a wider range of titbits or if I need to buy wine when visiting friends as organic wine is not available in most off-licences yet. I also try to ensure that nothing I buy contain-genetically modified ingredients, as I do not want to personally fund the industry with my consumer spending.

Over 2.8 million tonnes of artificial chemical pesticides, worth over $25 billion, are sprayed on the land every year worldwide. Over 3 million people worldwide are poisoned by such pesticides each year and over 220,000 people are killed, according to the World Health Organization (WHO). Many of the chemicals approved for use as pesticides in the US and European Union are associated with human carcinogenic and hormone-altering properties. The OECD reported that the United Kingdom uses more chemicals to grow food than in any other major industrialised country – more than twice the OECD average. It feels really good to realise that by buying my organic food from Green Ventures, I am ensuring that I am part of the solution to this problem and not adding to it.

Hopefully, you will want to be part of the solution too. Look through the list below and see which changes you can start with this week. You may not notice any immediate change in your own health, but the health of our precious environment will certainly start to benefit and eventually you will too. Each positive change in our culture is brought about by individuals altering their personal habits until more and more people join in, and then suddenly the transformation builds a momentum that is unstoppable. Working individually and collectively, we truly can stop the destructive food culture that is currently putting at risk our children's inheritance as well as create a positive and nurturing food environment in its place.

How to score

3	if you do the suggestion nearly all the time
2	if you do it occasionally or fairly often
1	if you hardly ever do it
0	if you never do it

Suggestions that save you money

264 If your tap water is safe to use, drink tap water at home instead of bottled water.

If your household consumes two litre bottles per week, you can save enough to buy a couple of new pairs of jeans, not to mention the 104 non-biodegradable plastic-bottle mountain left behind.

265 Try to reduce the amount of meat you eat (if you're not vegetarian). The average meat consumption per person per annum in Nigeria is 6.4 kg (14.1 lb), China 23 kg (50.6 lb), Canada 65 kg (143 lb) and in the US 95 kg (209 lb).

Remember the large environmental footprint required to produce each kilogram of meat compared to vegetarian foodstuffs. Every kilogram of beef costs on average: 50–100,000 litres (13–26,000 US gallons) of water, 5,900 joules of energy, 145 kg (319 lb) in topsoil loss, 40 kg (88 lb) of manure, 11.5 kg (22 lb) of CO_2 equivalent, 10 kg (22 lb) grain, 200 mg of antibiotics and a range of pesticides. It takes six times the amount of land to feed a meat eater than it does to feed a vegetarian, but every little bit you cut down as a meat eater really helps the environment.

266 If you have access to a garden or a plot of land, grow some of your own food organically.

This is the ultimate in environmentally sustainable food.

267 If you don't have a garden, see if there are allotments available locally by contacting your council.

Allotments are small plots of land owned by local councils available for hire for fruit and vegetable production. In the UK ,rentals vary from the price of a couple of bottles of wine to the equivalent of four pairs of jeans annually, depending on your local council. An average plot if tended to properly can produce enough vegetables for an average family for nine months of the year, organically, locally grown and almost free.

268 If you are addicted to canned soft drink, try switching to concentrated bottled juice. There are even organic options now available, many of which are really delicious.

They cost far less than cans per litre of drink and are a healthier option, better for the environment and will even reduce the weight of your shopping. At the very minimum, ensure that aluminium cans end up being recycled, as they are one of the most energy-wasteful products in our bins. By choosing a concentrate, you reduce the need for packing and transport by up to five-sixths.

269 If you have access to the countryside or local open spaces, learn to harvest the treasures of wild foods such as blackberries, crab apples, wild garlic, dandelion leaves, nettles and wild rocket.

While they will save you money, taste delicious and are fully organic, they also save on food miles.

270 If you have a baby, try to breastfeed them from birth if possible.

This not only ensures that the baby receives all of the benefits of the food designed for it by nature, but also eliminates the energy, resources and packaging that goes into the production of baby foods and of course means that you don't have to spend your money on such unnecessary products.

Suggestions that cost nothing

271 Buy only GM-free foods.

This helps protect the rights of future generations to eat GM-free food and reduces the risks to the future of our environment.

272 Buy locally produced food.

This reduces the contribution food miles make to global warming and helps to create a market for organic, locally produced foods.

273 Check out if there is a local farmers market where you can buy good quality local produce.

Helps reduce food miles.

274 Buy fresh produce that can be eaten without refrigeration.

275 If you can't avoid using takeaway foods, see if they will allow you to bring your own reusable containers.

This reduces the waste mountain.

276 Get your potatoes delivered in the old-fashioned large brown paper sacks.

Reduces packaging waste to zero if bag is composted.

277 Buy individual oranges in preference to cartons of juice.

This not only eliminates unnecessary waste and processing involved in producing cartons of orange juice but also reduces the need for the excessive fruit plantations required for our colossal consumption. These plantations are yet another pressure on our remaining wildlife habitats in many countries. One fresh orange a day is plenty, yet juiced up we end up consuming far more than we would whole oranges.

278 If shopping in a supermarket, only buy cereals and rice (and other such products) that do not come double packed with an unnecessary box as well as a plastic bag.

Reduces the waste mountain and the weight you have to carry home.

279 Reduce the amount of fish you consume or better still stop eating fish.

The world's ocean fisheries are being decimated by huge factory ships, which leave a devastated seabed in their wake. If everybody seriously reduced their intake of fish, then our children and their children would have a better chance of having the joy of seeing seals, dolphins and walruses.

280 If you do eat fish, avoid the particular species of fish that are currently being overfished. These over-exploited stocks include Atlantic swordfish, wild Atlantic salmon and North Sea cod.

Many of these take a long time to reach breeding age and so stocks have been decimated very rapidly. By not buying them, you are helping to give them a chance to recover in the wild.

281 Also try to avoid fish such as tuna that involve the death of a whole range of other unwanted fish and sea mammals.

It is now estimated that over 26-million tonnes of unwanted species of fish and other sea creatures are captured annually in fishing nets and thrown back overboard dead.

282 Avoid factory-farmed fish.

Caging fish is unnatural and cruel. Fish are meant to explore the seas, not to spend their entire lives caged in a couple of metres of water. It leads to high rates of disease, and the use of many toxic chemicals in a vain attempt to control this.

Suggestions that cost a small amount extra

283 Join an organic box scheme and have mixed bags of organic fruit, vegetables and other organic produce delivered to your home.

You should be able to find a scheme that suits you on the internet. Weekly delivery prices for a mixed box start around the cost of a nice bottle of wine.

284 If you are not already buying any organic produce due to cost, promise yourself to buy one organic product each time you shop to get started.

In researching this item, I bought a basket of basic essentials from a supermarket in London to compare costs. The basket included a pint of milk, 250 g (8.8 oz) of butter, 500 g (17.6 oz) of brown sugar, 500 g (17.6 oz) of corn-flakes and a 800g 28.2 oz) loaf of white bread. The organic basket cost £4.10

(5.90 or $7.50). The ordinary food raised using artifical pes-
ticides and fertilisers cost £3.70 (5.30 or $6.70). Now ask
yourself, could you not afford the extra 40p per week to switch
your basics to organic products? This is only 60 extra Euro cents
or 80 US cents per week, which after all is only the equivalent
of a bag of crisps. By the way, the organic cornflakes were
actually cheaper than the mainstream brand at the supermarket.

**285 If your family is on a tight budget and so can't afford
to buy organic food for everyone, start buy buying organic
baby food first.**
This means that your baby will start life not being exposed to
a cocktail of pesticides, artificial flavourings, preservatives and
colourings.

286 Buy local honey.
Reduces food miles even if usually a little bit more expensive
than mass-produced honey and you can also return the jars
when finished for reuse.

**287 If you are a meat eater, don't buy factory-farmed
chicken, pâté de foie gras or veal.**
There are some companies that produce cruelty-free veal and
pâté de foie gras. Look out for their labels.

**288 If you buy tuna, please ensure that it is certified from
a dolphin-friendly source. Thousands of dolphins die each
year needlessly in inappropriate netting used to harvest
tuna from our seas.**

**289 Buy free-range or even better free-range organic
meat if you do buy meat.**
At my local supermarket organic free-range chicken is about
twice the price of a factory-farmed chicken. This admittedly is
expensive but you are paying for a clear conscience. If you feel

*that you cannot afford it, think about having chicken less often
and buying organic with the amount you save.*

290   Buy a seed sprouter and produce your own delicious
fresh vitamin and enzyme rich sprouts. These are multi-sto-
ried plastic containers with pores. You place dried beans
and seeds such as mung beans, peas, alfalfa seeds etc in
each of the three layers. You then pour a little water over
them each day and within approximately a week you have
your very own delicious sprouts, saving all that plastic
packaging from the supermarket.

*These cost approximately the price of three bottles of wine for
a three-layer combination which allows you to sprout three different seeds but they will provide you with a lifetime of nutri-
tious, vitamin rich natural food. I often sprout dried marrowfat
peas, chickpeas and alfalfa sprouts, with the sprouted mar-
rowfats being one of my favourites. You can buy 250 g (8.8 oz)
bags of organic alfalfa seeds or 500 g (17.6 oz) of organic
dried chickpeas for the price of half a litre of wine.*

Suggestions that require a significant capital investment

291   If your family is unnecessarily fussy about drinking
tap water install a water purifier on your drinking tap. A
cheaper method is to use a water jug with a filter.

*A plumbed-in water purifier can cost about the price of a small
fridge. The filter cartridge needs to be changed every six months
and they cost the same as a reasonable pair of jeans. Both
methods eliminate the need for mountains of plastic bottles but
involve the use of materials in the manufacture and packaging
of the purifier and the filter cartridges.*

Other suggestions

1 _____ ☐

2 _____ ☐

3 _____ ☐

4 _____ ☐

5 _____ ☐

_____

	Year 1	Year 2	Year 3	Year 4	Year 5
Suggestions Score (subtotal)					

Chapter 7
Home and Personal Maintenance

If you have ever passed a house that is being refurbished or has new residents moving in, you will notice the huge amount of waste generated and an accompanying expenditure of energy and resources. This will also often include discarded wood, old furniture and unwanted objects. Even if you are not buying or moving into a new property, the maintenance and decoration of your home is where you can have a significant impact on the environment. Decorating materials are probably the largest source of toxic chemicals that most individuals will come across in their day-to-day lives. Today's paints, inks and adhesives are made from a host of synthetic chemicals, mostly derived from various petrochemicals. In the manufacturing process, over 25 tonnes of waste per tonne of paint is created. Often the solvents they contain are carcinogenic, cause respiratory diseases and are damaging to crops and wildlife.

Furniture is the largest product that we will buy for our homes, and it too has an environmental price attached. Mahogany-wood production is probably the most well known example – it is estimated that one hectare of rainforest has to be cut down to log just one mahogany tree. However, many other materials used in furniture making – such as plastics, metals, glass, glues and solvents – also have an impact. This includes the energy used in extraction and production, along with the pollutants released during manufacture. Many people don't realise that a lot of today's synthetic decorating materials and furniture continue to emit small amounts of chemicals into the surrounding air for years while they are still 'in use'.

People living far away from our homes often pay the price for our goods. The land of the Yanomami in Brazil, for example, is becoming increasingly polluted with toxic mercury as a result of illegal mining. The spiritual home of the Amungme tribe in Indonesia is being devastated by copper and gold mining. Across the globe, native people's homelands are being polluted in the name of finding evermore oil to satisfy our guzzling automobiles. It is very easy to put all the blame on the Rio Tinto Zincs, the Exxons, the greedy Brazilian miners, but they would not be there if our consumer lifestyles did not demand satisfaction at all costs. While we may disagree with the actions of these corporations, they are only satisfying the markets created by our wasteful consumerism. However, I really believe in people's essential decency. I believe that, once people learn about what is being done in their name, they will start to change – a gentle revolution is emerging, of which this book is a small part.

The best approach to these issues, first of all, is to question whether you really need to do whatever decorating, refurbishment or building you are planning. If the answer is yes, then you need to ask what the most environmentally benign method of doing so is. When my then partner and I bought our cottage ten years ago, we naturally needed all the usual furniture for it. There was already a fitted kitchen which, while not being my first choice of design, was perfectly adequate to our needs. So why throw it out? If you really can't stand the previous owner's taste in colours, you can buy new doors f or fitted cupboards. The double bed, dining-room table and chairs came from our previous flats and the sofa bed was bought from a friend of a friend. The desk and filing cabinets for my office were found at a second-hand furniture specialist. The only new items of furniture that we bought were the fridge and washing machine, as we wanted to use the most environmentally efficient on the market.

Another example of questioning the need for action in the first place is my front-garden's picket fence. I fell into fits of laughter one day when a neighbour knocked on my front door and asked if I knew my fence was on the pavement? I came out and there it was, lying like a line of fainted soldiers along the pavement. I quickly cleared it up but it was too rotten to repair, so my thoughts turned to how to buy a new fence. My first thought was to buy a fence made from recycled plastic. This would not only help provide a market for recycled plastic, but would avoid the need to use fresh timber. The thought that I would never have to paint it again was also appealing. However, then I thought why replace it at all? The fence was in front of a privet hedge, so I decided there was actually no need to replace the fence at all as the hedge served the same purpose equally well.

When refurbishing, it is crucial to think through what is the best environmental practice, as very often decisions taken will have consequences for years to come. For example, a white bathroom suite can be far harder to keep clean, requiring a higher use of cleaning materials for its lifetime than you might otherwise need. Similarly, if you are replacing an old door or window, choosing a double-glazed replacement will save heating energy for its entire lifetime.

I recently had to replace a door. I had been burgled twice within a couple of weeks and the second burglar smashed my back door and the whole thing had to be replaced. The door company presumed that I would want a new PVC door. I had replaced a damaged window in the mid-1990s with a double-glazed unit made from PVC, thinking at the time that it was the best environmental solution. Luckily, since then I had read about the toxic hazards posed by PVC both in its manufacture and disposal. Besides producing a large amount of toxic waste in its production, it is a poorer insulation material than wood and if burnt in a household fire it emits hydrogen chloride gas, dioxins and phosgene, leading to even greater health risks from domestic fires. And the bad news for PVC does not even stop there. PCV in landfill emits toxic plasticisers and other heavy metals. Not willing to have this on my conscience, I ordered a wooden replacement door with a double-glazed unit inserted.

The same is true for when you go out to buy cleaning or decorating materials. Make an effort to buy the environmentally best available option. There are detergents and laundry liquids that are made totally from organic materials, and there are paints and wood-treatment products that are far more natural than the synthetic formulas that currently flood our DIY shop shelves. These are usually far more biodegradable, lead to lower energy emissions and are far less polluting. Many products use citrus oils (made from citrus fruits) to replace the more toxic synthetic solvents. There is a whole range of more natural wood treatments available too, but you often don't need to treat internal timbers at all if the atmospheric environment is properly maintained. The WHO report that decorators are 40-percent more likely to contract lung diseases than the general population. So next time you are paying someone to decorate your home, please see if you can afford to buy them the more benign decorating materials. I used a white natural organic undercoat and gloss paints when re-painting the woodwork inside my house and it's just as good as the petrochemical-based paint. The only difference I found was that it took longer to dry out fully, but the fact my house was free of noxious fumes more than made up for this slight inconvenience.

These principles also apply when refurbishment is planned at your workplace or any organisations you are involved with. There is a lot of stress involved for management, not only in organising people to carry out the refurbishment or redecoration, but also in trying to ensure that the normal day to day running is not unduly disrupted. This often means that they may not take the time to think about the environmental consequences of what is planned. But it is really one of the most crucial times for the environmental impact to be considered, because the consequences can last for decades. Closing windows and doors in winter to keep the heat in is important, but it will have only a fraction of the effect of ensuring that the new heating system being installed is the most energy-efficient model available. Similarly, having a policy of turning off the lights when they are not in use is important, but of far more significance is the decision about what lights to install in the first place if a refurbishment is taking place. If they are energy guzzlers, then they will guzzle for every day of their lives.

I happened to be on the finance and administrative committee of an organisation I was a member of when their lease was up for renewal. I had joined that committee deliberately, as I thought it would be a useful place from which to influence an environmental agenda. As part of the renegotiations, the owners of the lease offered to refurbish the building. I suggested that we should obtain an environmental assessment of the refurbishment and I was delighted when my colleagues readily agreed to do so. The environmental consultant's report was quite in depth, covering everything from opportunities to purchase top quality second-hand furniture to recommendations for the most efficient type of heating system that would best suit the building.

Some aspects of the audit were implemented, such as sensor lights for the landings and toilets, and they ensured that all the new photocopying equipment was recycled-paper friendly. Other more ambitious recommendations – eg installing a grey-water system and a solar-energy system on the roof – are still in the pipeline. I have got permission to proceed with providing for solar power from the building's owners, but as it is a Grade One listed building getting permission from the planning authorities might be a little bit more delicate.

It is important to be gentle yet persistent when raising environmental issues at such times. Refurbishments can be incredibly stressful for management and being argumentative won't help get your message across (although I can't claim never to have lapsed into quarrelling myself). Try to supply examples of savings that can be achieved. For example, find out how much can be saved by installing energy-saving light bulbs. Alternatively, determine the amount of water that could be saved if they installed a waterless urinal and how much that would save them over ten years. This approach can help management take what you are saying more seriously. If they are replacing furniture, go and get examples of the price of second-hand office furniture yourself. You can even do it on the web. They will be shocked at the good quality available and how much they can save.

It is also important to address environmental issues in our own personal maintenance, including personal cleaning products and cosmetics. Many of these products also contain a range of synthetic chemicals, whose production and release into the environment pose many toxic threats to both human health and that of our wider environment.

Researchers at the Mount Sinai School of Medicine in New York, in collaboration with the Environmental Working Group, examined nine volunteers to see what chemicals were to be found in their bodies. An extraordinary total of 167 chemicals were found including industrial compounds, pollutants, and other chemicals in their blood and urine. This was despite the fact that they did not work in the chemical industry or live near an industrial plant. Of the 167 chemicals found, 76 of them cause cancer in humans or animals, 94 are toxic to the brain and nervous system, and 79 cause birth defects or abnormal development. Of course, it is also almost impossible to carry out research into all the possible combinations and permutations that such chemicals may cause through their interactions within our bodies.

It makes sense to reduce the chemical cocktail that we expose our bodies to daily, and a significant route for chemicals into our bodies is through our skin. This is especially relevant to the cosmetics and personal-cleaning products that are sold in their billions across the globe. Among the synthetic chemicals in common usage in cosmetics are isobutyl paraben, an oestrogen mimic which is used in deodorants and moisturisers; triclosan which forms dioxins when burnt; xylene, a liver-damaging substance that is used in lacquers and nail polishes; alkylphenol ethoxylates, which is used in shampoos and hair-dyes and which is also a hormone disrupter and toxic to fish; and acetone, which is used in nail-polish remover and which is a lung irritant.

In an article about the toxic chemicals used in shampoos, the *Ecologist* magazine listed the ingredients of one of Procter & Gamble's highest selling shampoos called 'Clairol Herbal Essences' as containing: cocamidopropyl betaine, methyl and propyl paraben, diazolidinyl urea, benzoic acid, DMDM – hydantoin, cocamide monoethanolamine, sodium lauryl sulphate, propylene glycol, tetrasodium EDTA, synthetic chemical colourants (chemical composition notlisted): CI 17200, CI 15510, CI 160730, CI 142053, and synthetic chemical parfum (chemical composition not listed). This is not exactly the natural herbal product most people thought they were buying. In addition, most top-selling cosmetics, perfumes and deodorants contain phthalates, which is a family of synthetic chemicals hazardous to human health and reproduction. They are used to provide flexibility and to dissolve other ingredients. They are readily absorbed through the skin and are associated with birth defects, organ damage, infertility and cancer. Over a million tonnes of these chemicals are produced in western Europe every year. Supermarket and mainstream brands of toothpastes similarly contain a list of synthetic chemicals and additives such as artificial sweeteners and preservatives including triclosan, polyvinyl methyl ether, maleic acid, rhodanide and fluoride.

So what can we do about this extraordinary cocktail of chemicals with which we are daily assaulting our bodies? We can cut down or eliminate their use or we can choose to find alternatives that use natural products available in nature and which avoid the use of this huge array of synthetic chemicals. Many tribal peoples use no such products whatsoever and yet they maintain healthy skin simply using pure clean water. There are now however a whole range of cosmetics and toiletries available that are genuinely based on natural products. The web is still probably the easiest way to track down local suppliers of such products. Alternatively, your health-food store might be another rich resource of such locally-made products or might know where you can buy some. It seems bizarre that we are willing to smear substances on our bodies that we would not dream of putting near our stomachs. The list below makes a number of suggestions on how to change your personal maintenance products. I think that you will be pleasantly surprised with the difference when you switch to more natural products.

Check out the list below too for suggestions on how to take care of the environment while you are taking care of your home. Remember, a lot of the decisions you make on the issues below may be with you for years to come. A single pesticide-sprayed apple is eaten only once, but if you choose a sofa that is slowly leaking toxic chemicals into your living room it may be leaking those chemicals for your entire life. So stop and think before you buy. Happy decorating!

How to score

3   if you do the suggestion nearly all the time

2   if you do it occasionally or fairly often

1   if you hardly ever do it

0   if you never do it

Suggestions that save you money

292 Where possible, choose second-hand furniture rather than buying new items.

Often second-hand furniture has a charm some new items lack. After all, they are just younger versions of what later gets termed 'antique'. I have been amazed at the wonderful bargains that are available in used furniture.

293 Try refurbishing old or broken furniture rather than throwing it out.

Simply having the coverings replaced can save a significant amount of money and the furniture will still look as good as new.

294 If you want to redecorate a fitted kitchen, see if you can just replace the cupboard doors instead of throwing whole units out lock, stock and barrel.

There are hardware stores and internet companies that now offer a whole range of new doors for cupboards and drawers with prices from about the same as only two bottles of wine for new cupboard doors and the price on one good bottle of wine for the drawer fronts. As well as avoiding scrapping the infrastructure of your fitted kitchen, you can save a very large amount of money.

295 If building a new bathroom, buy your new fittings from architectural rescue shops. Wonderful old sinks, baths

and toilets are available from junk shops, which will add real character to your decor.

This not only saves the energy and resources used to manufacture new products but it will often be considerably cheaper. Remember, however, to ensure that you attach water spray attachments to the taps to save water.

296 If you need curtains, see if you can buy them second-hand.

You might find a quality of curtain away above your budget while avoiding even more waste in our landfills.

297 Repair your shoes rather than throwing them away.

Shoes can often be resoled or re-heeled and last up to another year for a fraction of the cost of a new pair of shoes. Sometimes all that is wrong is that the inner-soles have broken down. Pairs of these can be bought from most shoe shops for the price of a cheap bottle of wine, and they just slip into the shoe with no glue or anything else required, and can help prolong the life of perfectly good shoes for another 6 to 12 months.

298 Mend your clothes rather than simply throwing them away.

'A stitch in time saves nine' is still absolutely true. Simply taking out your needle and thread when the first button loosens or when thread runs will ensure that the garment lasts a lot longer.

299 Use vinegar mixed with water to replace chemical-based window cleaner.

If you add five parts water to one part organic vinegar in a reused spray-bottle, the cost works out at less than a third of the cost of a major supermarket brand.

300 Brushing the toilet for a brief minute daily will seriously reduce the need for chemical toilet cleaners.

Ordinary toilet cleaner costs about the equivalent of three packets of crisps per litre. As I give my toilet a regular, good brushing, I find that a litre of an environmentally friendly brand now lasts me up to two years.

301 Buy washing-up liquid and washing machine liquid or powder in bulk.

This eliminates waste plastic bottles/packaging and can often be substantially cheaper.

302 Use washable dishcloths rather than kitchen paper. If you have to buy kitchen paper (I have never found I need it in my kitchen), always buy the recycled option.

Using reusable cloths instead of throwaway kitchen paper will save you money in the medium to long term. Virgin paper towels cost the same as the recycled option in my local supermarket, again showing that the green option does not have to be more expensive.

303 Use clean rags made from old sheets and clothes etc instead of new bought cleaning cloths.

Homemade cloths will cost you nothing except a couple of seconds with the scissors.

304 If buying a new vacuum cleaner, ensure you buy a bagless model.

This will save you wasting money unnecessarily on disposable bags for the lifetime of the machine, saving you approximately the price of a new vacuum cleaner.

305 If you already have a carpet cleaner that does use bags, you can buy permanent vacuum bags that you can use over and over again. You simply empty and replace them in the machine.

These cost approximately the price of three bottles of wine but you will never have to buy another disposable vacuum cleaner bag again. You can empty your vacuum cleaner into the compost bin if your carpets are made from natural materials. If they include synthetic fibres they won't decay, so need to be disposed of in your regular waste bin.

306   If you need a new set of crockery, consider buying a second-hand set.

You are not only helping create a market for reused crockery, which saves the energy and clay used in their manufacture, but they can bring an added charm to your home that brand-new crockery is unable to.

307   If you need new clothes, visit second-hand clothes shops in the better part of town and you will find some real gems – maybe of better quality that you might normally be able to afford.

As well as the bonuses of knowing you are helping to avoid new waste and having a new wardrobe at a fraction of the normal cost, you'll have the added bargain of not having to worry about the ethics of the company making the article.

308   Avoid buying clothes that need to be dry-cleaned.

The solvent used in most dry-cleaning establishments is perchloroethylene which is quite toxic. It is also far cheaper to wash clothes at home than to take them to be dry-cleaned every time they are dirty.

309   If you need wood for DIY around the house, check nearby rubbish skips or see if there is a reclaimed wood supplier in your neighbourhood.

This not only saves trees but can add an unexpected aesthetic to your work. There is a list of UK reclaimed wood suppliers at www.recycle.mcmail.com/timbrec. Check of course that the wood is disease free.

310 Rather than throwing out your old pot-pourri, you can revive it by buying a little bottle of flower oils. Place the pot pourri in a plastic bag and sprinkle on a few drops of the oil. Seal with an elastic band and leave it for two days to soak up the fragrance, and you'll have a fully revived fragrance for your home.

A small bottle of natural floral oil costs only about the price of a half litre of wine and will revive your pot-pourri for many years. There is a large range of wonderful natural floral smells to choose from.

311   Use less cosmetics. If you put on make-up every day, try having one cosmetic-free day a week and see how it feels.

The less you wear means less pollution will arise from its formulation, less packaging will get dumped and the more money you'll have for things that are good for you.

Suggestions that cost nothing

312 Don't buy any unsustainably-produced mahogany.
Often over an acre of precious habitat-rich rainforest is destroyed to get at one mahogany tree. This is a dreadful and unnecessary carnage.

313 Do not buy any uncertified rainforest products for your home.
International certification schemes such as the FSC ensure that the wood that you buy is from sustainable sources and is not the result of rainforest or ancient woodland destruction.

314 Use non-petroleum based hand-cleaning products such as a natural hand cleaner that is made with hemp oil. It removes oil, grease, paint etc safely.

I found some for the price of a bottle of wine for 500 g (17.6 oz) from the Hemp Shop on the net.

315 If you need outdoor wood protection, you can now get a chemical-free all-weather wood protector made from natural asphalt and organic ingredients.

Many of the current commercial wood preservatives contain very toxic chemicals.

316 If you need a tradesperson such as a plumber or carpenter, find someone who is based locally. You could also join the local green-currency system and see if there is anyone there who can help you.

Hiring local people reduces the amount of congestion and pollution due to unnecessary travel.

317 Use houseplants such as spider plants to help clean your air of chemical pollutants by aborbing them.

Spider plants reproduce so easily that you should be able to get one for free.

318 Rather than using nasty aerosol chemical based airfresheners – use fresh air instead or buy some pot-pourri.

Pot-pourri is a mixture of dried aromatic flowers and leaves impregnated with natural floral oils and costs the equivalent of only three bags of crisps per 50 g (1.8 oz) bag – roughly the same cost as a can of chemical air-freshener. The pile of empty pressurised cans are left for posterity, whereas the potpourri will decay naturally if thrown on the compost heap when used.

319 Use lemon juice instead of bleach for your clothes etc. □
Traditional chlorine-based bleach is extremely damaging to the environment.

320 Rather than buying fabric freshener, use dried-lavender or lavender-wax beads in your clothes cupboards to keep your clothes smelling naturally sweet. □
Dispenses with the need for the synthetic chemicals used in the manufacture of fabric fresheners.

321 Use baking soda instead of supermarket brands of scouring substances for cleaning your kitchen sink, bathtub and oven. □
Baking soda, which is far more benign than the synthetic chemical-based supermarket formulas, will not scratch sensitive porcelain ware.

323 Grate soap into hot water with some baking powder to replace floor-cleaning substances. For rinsing after washing the floor, you could add some vinegar. □
Avoids chemical-based floor cleaners.

324 If your home has soft water, you can use liquid soap for washing clothes, but if your local water supply is hard, and has a high level of minerals dissolved in it which make it harder for the soap to foam and clean your clothes, you will have to use more detergents. □
If the latter choose biodegradable detergents without artificial perfumes.

325 If you add a teaspoon of clove or tea-tree oil to a quarter of a litre of water and put it in a spray bottle, it acts as a natural fungicide. This can naturally clean your shower curtain if it gets mouldy. □

326 Instead of using bleach to remove deodorant stains ☐
from under the arms of shirts, blouses, t-shirts etc, rub with
white vinegar and then wash as normal.

327 Always buy recycled toilet paper. Using precious virgin ☐
paper to simply clean our bums is really not necessary.

*In my local supermarket recycled luxury toilet-paper costs slightly
less than the toilet paper made from virgin paper, although the
price differential differs from shop to shop. You often have to
read the small print though to find out the source of the paper.
By buying recycled loo-paper, you are helping to create a market
for the paper that you recycle. There is no point in recycling if
there is no market for the goods collected.*

328 If buying twine for use around the house, avoid plastic: ☐
stick to the traditional hemp or other natural-fibre twines.

Hemp will decompose naturally after disposal in your compost heap.

329 Avoid silk and fur clothing. ☐

*Silk is made from silk moths, which are suffocated to produce
the silk. Each kilogram of silk requires 30 kg (66 lb) of mulberry
leaf on which the silk larvae feed. Fur farms involve cruelly locking up often over 75,000 wild animals in tiny cages for their
entire lives. Disposal of the large amounts of waste products
resulting from the unnatural concentration of animals creates
serious environmental problems.*

330 Recycle any old unwanted furniture rather than ☐
throwing it away. If unable to find a buyer, try simply leaving it outside your home for an evening with a note on it
saying that it is unwanted. Alternatively, there are plenty of
second-hand furniture shops and charities who collect furniture for people in need.

Reduces the waste mountain.

331   Recycle your old clothes, sheeting etc. If they are not good enough for the charity shop, drop them off at a charity-recycling collection point if one is available.

They are able to reuse the fibres as a raw material for other products if the clothing itself isn't good enough to be sold.

332   When choosing underlay for a new carpet, there are really good ones now available made from 100-per-cent recycled post consumer waste.

These cost no more than the traditional makes but of course contribute to creating a market for recycled materials.

333   When buying shampoo avoid products with synthetic preservatives, petrochemicals and artificial perfumes.

Many companies selling such products can be found easily on the internet and cost roughly the same as mainstream chemical based products.

334   Avoid using nail polish. You can have shiny nails by instead using a fine pumice stone and following it up with moisturising cream.

Nail polish often contains toluene (toxic), formaldehyde (can trigger asthma symptoms and is a carcinogen) and dibutyl phthalate (a hormone disrupter).

335   If you do use nail polish, buy natural nail polish remover.

The regular nail-polish remover usually contains acetone (which irritates the lungs and is toxic if ingested) or ethyl acetate (damages the central nervous system and the environment).

336   If you do use a deodorant, buy natural deodorants that do not contain formaldehyde.

337   If you use a skin moisturiser, avoid those that contain hormone-disrupting phthalates.

338   Use non-toxic suntan lotions.

The list of synthetic chemicals that we smear on our poor skins under the name of suntan lotions is extraordinary. One main-stream brand of suntan oil I recently bought contained the following: dicaprylyl ether, alkyl benzoate, caprylic triglyceride, cyclomethcone, 4-methylbenzylidene camphor, tocopheryl acetate, butyl methoxydibenzoylmethane, lanolin alcohol, par-fum and paraffinum liquidum. Natural suntan lotions and screens are available in the UK from companies such as Natures Way, or internationally you can buy Urtekram on the net from www.tlcinabottle.co.uk. One brand of sunscreen, which contains only vegetable ingredients, costs the same as the chemical brands and is free from aluminium and titanium dioxide. The range covers sunscreen factors 9, 14 and 24. The after-sun lotion costs are also comparable to the chemical versions.

Suggestions that cost a small amount extra

339   If you don't want to buy second-hand furniture, you can buy new furniture made from recycled/reclaimed wood.

While not necessarily cheaper, the reclaimed look can often be very beautiful.

340   Use organic paints in preference to oil-based chemical paints.

Organic white paint costs about twice the price of chemical-based paints per litre, but as the paint is only required every four years or so it is worth the extra amount to ensure you are not breathing in noxious fumes any time you occupy the room being painted.

341   If hiring decorators for your home, find one who is committed to using environmentally-sound materials.

This makes it easier to negotiate environmental best practice in

*what you want done, as they will be familiar with the issues
involved and will better-know local sources of environmentally
sustainable decorating products.*

**342 If hiring an architect to design an extension, refurbish-
ment or new home, find one who is knowledgeable about
environmental best practice.**

*Their expertise will be invaluable in ensuring that it is done in
the best possible way for the environment. This investment will
pay off for the entire lifetime of the room or home.*

**343 Use plant based turpentine in preference to chemical-
based products.**

**344 For the rare times you need a liquid toilet cleaner,
buy an environmentally-responsible brand. The same
applies to sink-cleaning materials.**

*They can cost roughly twice that of a supermarket brand but as
you only have to buy it occasionally, it works out at roughly only
the cost of half a litre of wine per year for the sake of a clear
conscience. They often use lemon juice as a base, which may
be bitter but is obviously biodegradable and definitely non-toxic.*

**345 Use only environmentally-friendly washing-up liquid
and washing-machine products.**

*Many household cleaners contain phosphates, which while not
being toxic to humans cause significant environmental problems
in watercourses after being poured down the sink. They can
cause rapid growth of algae, which can consume all the available oxygen, leaving none for the rest of the river wildlife including the fish that are dependent on the oxygen dissolved in the
water for survival.*

**346 Use beeswax as furniture polish rather than the
synthetic-spray can versions.**

Admittedly, it takes a little more elbow grease but it smells nice and you know you are not adding any further noxious substances into your home atmosphere. A mainstream brand of synthetic spray polish costs about half the price of a tin of silicon-free beeswax in natural gum turpentine. But like the other cleaning products, the price is low to begin with and the small extra cost is spread over a long period of time. The tin is also easily recycled whereas the synthetic spray can is made up of a range of substances that make it very difficult to recycle.

347   Use natural toothpaste, which avoids the use of chemicals found in most supermarket brands of toothpaste, such as fluoride, silica, artificial chemical sweeteners and triclosan (a chlorinated aromatic compound) and uses natural cleaners instead such as chalk and lemon juice.

Natural toothpaste costs about the price of a packet of crisps more than the supermarket brand per 75 ml tube, so avoiding unnecessary chemicals.

348   Ensure that the space around all the piping and ducts leading from the outside of your home are properly sealed.

While costing very little, this can eliminate a significant source of heat loss.

349   If you need to buy new glasses, buy from the new ranges of glassware that are now made from post-consumer recycled glass.

A range on the net included tumblers and wine glasses that cost approximately the cost of one bottle of wine and a tall glass jug, the price of two bottles of wine.

350   If you would like to go one further, then buy from a range of wine glasses and tumblers that are ingeniously made from reused glass bottles.

These save even the energy formerly used to melt recycled bottles.

351 When re-stocking stationery, always consider the recycled ranges first.

352 If you want to buy new clothes rather than second-hand clothes, for an environmentally-sound alternative, consider the range of clothes now made from organically-produced cotton.

Cotton production is the world's most polluting crop. While it uses approximately two per cent of the world's agricultural land, it uses up more than 25 per cent of the world's annual consumption of pesticides and artificial fertilisers. This is because it is grown in vast mono-cultural plantations. You can travel for hours in Texas and see only cotton plants out your bus window. Organic cotton clothes are still between 20 and 50-per-cent more expensive than regular pesticide-grown cotton products but you can occasionally get them on sale, which can bring them down to more usual prices. There are a number of net-based companies selling ranges of organic clothes and bed linen, cotton underwear and clothing for children and babies. If you can afford it, go for it; you will know your clothes are then part of the answer and not the problem.

353 Buy naturally dyed wool or, even better, buy undyed woollen products.

Wool is usually dyed with metallic dyes, which are polluting when they get into water sources.

354 As well as seeing if you can hire a local tradesperson for building or other domestic work, try to find one who is environmentally responsible. See if there is a green guide in your area with listings of services.

Environmentally aware trades -people will be able to advise you on environmental best practice. They will also use environmentally-friendly materials and correctly recycle waste.

355 Avoid use of toxic batteries if at all possible, and if you have to use batteries, use rechargeable ones, some of which can be recharged using solar-panel rechargers.

You can get both solar-powered and mains-electricity-powered battery rechargers, both of which cost about the price of a cheap pair of jeans. Many of them can recharge a wide range of regular domestic battery sizes. Over time, you will be able to recoup your investment in the recharger and also eliminate toxic-waste batteries from your rubbish. It is worth noting that while batteries are among the most toxic products in your home, they are very easily recycled, so do find out how to recycle them. Most local authorities have a battery-recycling point somewhere in their area. Check on their website to find out. If they do not, a neighbouring council might have such a facility.

356 Buy sustainably-produced wooden toys for children instead of plastic toys.

More often than not they last far longer and can be passed down to younger children or even the next generation. Plastic toys use up non-renewable petro-chemicals and some soft plastic toys contain toxic phthalates.

357 If you have a new baby in the family, many items you will need for a short period of time such as go-karts, cots or even toys are readily available second-hand. Check your local classified adverts or exchange magazines. Don't forget to sell or pass them on when you are finished with them yourself.

This will save you money and precious resources and reduce waste to landfill/incineration.

358 If you do feel you need to use cosmetics, try to buy products that are based on natural materials rather than synthetic chemicals.

Many cosmetics contain a range of synthetic chemicals, which are often on recognised lists of toxic substances, for instance, parabens, phthalates, Toluene or alkylphenol ethoxylates. Avoiding their use reduces your own personal exposure and reduces the amount of these substances released into the wider environment.

359 You can take the step of using natural cosmetics even further by seeking out such cosmetic products that use organically-certified raw materials.

These will sometimes cost a bit more than the usual chemical-based products, but as you do not buy them every week, are well worth the extra investment.

360 If buying a new quilt or pillows for your bed, find a quilt filled with natural products such as un-dyed sheep's wool or duck down.

These do cost considerably more than the artificially filled quilts but you can luxuriate in the knowledge that you are kept warm naturally while asleep.

Suggestions that require a significant capital investment

361 If your house has floorboards, consider installing insulation underneath, or at least seal the gaps between the timbers. Fire-resistant insulation materials made from recycled newspapers are now on the market.

This will save heat loss in winter by up to ten per cent.

362 Buy natural floor coverings. There is now a range of natural floor coverings such as non-chemically treated pure wool carpets. Sisal and coir are traditional floor coverings from abroad that are now becoming increasingly available in Europe.

While pure wool carpets are more expensive than those made from synthetic materials, you have the satisfaction of knowing that no toxic chemicals were used in their manufacture. If they are too expensive for your budget, try for the highest percentage of wool content that you can afford.

363 If you are building or renovating your home or workplace, consult an expert on passive solar design.

Passive solar is a fancy name for using the natural heat of the sun to warm your home. For example, they recommend placing large double-glazed units on the south-facing walls of buildings to maximise the warmth from the sun for the home. Up to 50 per cent of the heating costs of a home can be reduced for the building's entire lifetime by the incorporation of such measures at the beginning at no extra cost. However, it is quite expensive to retrofit passive solar design concepts into a building after it has been built.

364 Similarly, simple, non-technological building techniques can be used to apply passive cooling for a building.

They simply maximise natural airflows through the building and shading systems in summer to maximise natures natural cooling systems, thus minimising any unnecessary energy usage. Again, like passive solar design, there is almost no extra cost if installed when the building is being built but are expensive to retrofit.

365 Consider a 'green roof' if building a new home.

This is a roof with soil on top, in which wildflowers and grass can grow. This provides wildlife habitats but also improves thermal and acoustic insulation.

366 If constructing a new home in the countryside, consider a beautiful earth building.

These reduce the impact on the landscape, the raw material is environmentally benign and they can also save between 30 and

60 per cent in energy costs compared to the traditional type of construction.

367 Alternatively, if you are building a new home, consider building a straw-bale home. □

As well as being a fraction of the cost of traditional buildings, they are really cosy, they provide excellent warmth and sound-insulating properties that can look beautiful. They simply use bales of tightly packed straw and then plaster over the bales, instead of stone or brick, so that the home looks like any other, except that it has wonderful thick walls. They can last up to 100 years and have excellent fire-resistant and earthquake-resistant capabilities.

Other suggestions

1 _____ □

2 _____ □

3 _____ □

4 _____ □

5 _____ □

	Year 1	Year 2	Year 3	Year 4	Year 5
Suggestions Score (subtotal)					

Chapter 8
Saving the Planet at Work

Greening your work life, as already discussed, is as important if not more so than greening your personal lifestyle. The possible environmental impact caused by a workplace usually far exceeds that of one individual person or family. Think for example of how your workplace's electricity bill compares to your home bill or the amount of waste produced at work compared to that produced by your own household.

This is not only because they are likely to have far more people located on the premises, with all their individual environmental payloads, but also workplaces are significant consumers of environmental resources and creators of significant amounts of physical waste in their own right. In Canada, commercial and industrial sectors use more than 43 per cent of all energy consumed in the country, compared to 18 per cent by households. In Japan, 78 million tonnes of waste are produced every year by the commercial sector compared to 50 million by people in their homes. Similarly, the UK disposes over 77 million tonnes of waste every year from shops, offices and factories, whereas homes dump just over 50 million tonnes. The British commercial sector also uses over 33 million tonnes of oil-equivalent in energy consumption every year, which is a large amount of energy in anybody's book.

All of the issues that we have already examined – such as water, energy, transport, waste, shopping – also apply to your workplace. How you go about greening your own work practise and the organisation that you work for can be a little different from how you green the rest of your life though. But the principles of how you negotiate with others to achieve this are often the same as you use when negotiating with your family or house mates. I have always tried to operate by two principles, with greater and lesser success depending on the situation over the years: first, that I must endeavour not to force my opinions about changes in lifestyle on to others and, second, that I will try to lead by example with what I do in my own life.

Bringing about change at work will often depend on where you are in the organisation's hierarchy. The higher up you are it is possibly more likely that you will have the authority to implement changes, but in my experience the key people responsible for making many crucial decisions about the environmental performance of a company can lie at all levels of a company. For instance, it is the cleaner not the managing director who normally decides whether or not to buy environmentally friendly cleaning products or recycled paper toilet paper.

I have worked in a number of mainly clerical and administrative jobs since being a professional ballet dancer. My key requirement has been flexibility to allow me the opportunity to pursue my various environmental and political projects, but in all of them I try to do what I can to green my own work life and seek to make a contribution to greening the organisation as a whole. In none of my workplaces to date have I been able to go as far as I have been able to as director of my local environmental charity or the national membership organisation of which I became the deputy chair of the board – in both of these I was in a position to introduce environmental auditing (as mentioned in Chapter 1) which significantly improved both organisations' environmental performance.

As the manager of a London council's local Chamber of Commerce, I persuaded them to start auditing how much of the

£20 million worth of goods and services that they bought annually was actually sourced from the local community. As well as wanting them to support the local businesses which comprised the membership of my Chamber, and which employed many of the council's own local residents, I also wanted to reduce the journey distances that goods and people had to travel before being utilised by the council. This would reduce carbon-dioxide emissions from transport and help reduce traffic congestion.

We commissioned specially designed envelope-reuse labels with the Chamber of Commerce's logo on it. We also ensured that we bought mainly manila envelopes, which are invariably made from recycled paper. Having consulted the other local business advice organisations that shared our open plan office with us, we were able to introduce an office wide paper-recycling scheme, which eliminated nearly 35 per cent of our waste stream at a stroke.

When a new government business organisation moved into the premises, they carried out a major refurbishment of the building. We wanted to ensure that environmental issues were taken into account. We got them to include a cycle parking bay in the new layout and a lighting system that allowed individual sections of the open-plan office to have individual switches. Our desks were beside a large bright window and so needed no artificial light on most days, but prior to the refurbishment it was linked in to the entire system and the lights had to be on all day. We were also able to ensure the spaces allocated for the paper-recycling storage bins were preserved in the new layout.

The biggest contradiction of the refurbishment was the installation of air-conditioning in the large basement meeting room area. The purpose of this was not to deal with the heat of summer but to mitigate the effect of the central-heating pipes passing through the meeting rooms in winter. It doubled the wasted energy. This brought home to me how crucial it is that the environment is thought about when refurbishment or building plans are being drawn up – they lay the groundwork for most of the future energy-consumption practices.

My next post was as a part-time accounts assistant for a children's charity. When I arrived there was no paper recycling at the office. I researched by phone and found a company that would collect our paper for free and persuaded the office manager to allow me to organise it. Most people now have a box at their desk for white paper and we recycle approximately six bags of top-quality white paper every three months. Having set this up, the office manager asked if they would recycle our magazine waste. We often have boxes of unused organisational magazines left over after distribution. The recycling company makes a small charge for collecting these, but it is well worth it.

After a couple of years, I decided to see if I could persuade the charity to convert to recycled paper for its photocopier. I researched the cost with various companies and discovered that the company that collected our paper had started selling the paper produced by the recycling mill. I thought this was a beautiful example of closing the loop, encompassing my ideal of life reflecting the natural waste cycles of the forest. The price quoted was cheaper than our then suppliers, so I sent off for a sample pack to show the office manager. The pack duly arrived and our office manager was surprised to see how good the quality was. The fact that it would save us approximately the equivalent of a couple of packets of crisps per ream helped win the argument.

We started ordering the new recycled paper and everything went well for around six months. However, I discovered the need for vigilance. One day I was in the photocopier room and was dismayed to find the latest paper delivery was non-recycled. I found out that the receptionist, to who the office manager had delegated responsibility for stationery ordering, had gone off and found an even cheaper price for non-recycled paper. I was a bit upset, and after some discussion she agreed she would return to the recycled product in future.

As a junior member of staff I try my best to keep out of office politics (I have plenty in my campaigning life outside of work), however, I was annoyed that we were going backwards. It is amazing how many people who support recycling the paper they've used need help in understanding that products made from recycled materials need to be bought as well, or nothing will actually be recycled. Anyway, five months later I noticed that another huge delivery of non-recycled paper had arrived. I am afraid I completely lost my cool and left the office to try to calm down. I had no financial reserves and no alternative job to go to and realised that I had broken my own rule about not forcing my values on to others. I returned sheepishly to the office, apologised and got on with things. I am relating this story in the hope that you will avoid falling into the trap I did. I recommend gentle persuasion, ensuring that your own actions are green and respecting the fact that others may not share your environmental priorities.

The nice end to this story is that the receptionist with whom I had become annoyed has become wonderfully proactive about recycling, on her own initiative researching and sorting out recycling for all our non-white office paper. This has nearly doubled the paper collected from the office and made a huge reduction in the weekly waste collection by the council. She is also one of the most enthusiastic volunteers to take our empty glass bottles over to the nearby bottle bank. She even ordered recycled white envelopes.

One of the more straightforward tasks was to sort out our energy supply. This was easier, as I pay the bills following authorisation. I got a blurb through the post from our electricity supplier after the government introduced the climate change levy (a tax on the CO_2 producing fuels used by businesses) stating that if we applied for the electricity company's green tariff we would be able to avoid the levy and our electricity would be slightly cheaper. A green tariff means that all the electricity supplied is sourced by the company from renewable-electricity sources, such as wind or solar energy. I did my sums and went to the office manager and successfully sold her the new deal. All that remained was to fill in the forms and send them off, so we have now been on a green electricity tariff for the last two years and saved a small amount of money for the charity at the same time.

I try and minimise my own energy use in the building by turning off my PC when I am not using it, even in lunch hours, and by regularly turning off lights and air-conditioning in rooms that are not being used. My desk is situated by the office window, which means that I do not have to have the office lights on for much of the time during daylight hours. As I recycle all my organic waste, white and coloured paper and glass, it means that the bin by my office desk is nearly always empty.

It is estimated that approximately 20 per cent of energy use in offices is now due to office equipment, with nearly two thirds of that used by PCs and monitors. Turning my PC and monitor off at lunchtime means that I save up to five hours electricity use over the week. Many cathode monitors use up to 120 watts per hour, which is the equivalent of over eight energy-saving bulbs. Research by the UK research institute BRECSU has found that a responsibly used and efficient PC can be run for about one-sixth of the electricity per year of non-efficient computers carelessly left on 24 hours a day. People also often forget that energy use by office equipment releases a large amount of waste heat, leading to overheated offices in summer and causing the air-conditioning to work even harder. A single PC and monitor alone can emit over 300 kilocalories of heat per hour.

I try not to pile all these suggested changes on my work colleagues all at the same time, but suggest them gradually over a number of years. It is important for me to remember that I am not a senior decision maker in the company, but just an ordinary member of staff. One of my latest projects at work was to tackle the water cooler. We had a plastic-bottle system, where once a month a water company delivered large blue bottles filled with filtered water for insertion in the water cooler. They were not only very heavy to lug around and therefore a health and safety risk, but they also took up a large amount of storage space.

I did some web research and then got out all my water-bottle invoices for the previous year. I found that we would save almost £750 per year by hiring an on-site water-filter cooling system. So armed, I again popped down to the office manager, who as she often ended up shifting the really heavy plastic bottles around was more than willing to hear the economic arguments. She got to work straight away, got a couple of quotes, and the new system was installed in approximately 20 minutes the following day. I hadn't laboured the environmental arguments with her, but the company salesman waxed lyrical about the truck journeys avoided and how much plastic was saved. He claimed that the heavy plastic bottles don't even last a year and there are huge skips full of waste plastic water bottles outside supply company plants.

So whatever position you hold in a company – office cleaner, chief executive or chair of the board – there are things that you can do to improve your company's environmental performance. Some will cost a little extra, some will actually save the company money and others will require long-term capital investment. So start thinking about the first small project you can suggest, and you will often be amazed how others will soon start responding positively. Good luck and remember not to force your actions on others but try by example and persuasion; otherwise you will waste too much emotional energy and not enjoy this process. Look at the list below and think of one action that you can start implementing this week.

How to score

3   if you do the suggestion nearly all the time

2   if you do it occasionally or fairly often

1   if you hardly ever do it

0   if you never do it

Suggestions that save your company money

368 Suggest commissioning an environmental audit of the firm's activities to identify potential savings and improved environmental practice.

Many US states offer various energy-efficiency grants to commercial companies, and the Federal Government and the European Union both also have grant programmes to help develop such technologies. If you live in the UK, your bosses might be interested to know that the government allows 100 per cent of the capital cost of water-saving measures to be written off against tax in their first year. This also applies to cars with low CO_2 emissions and energy-saving plant and machinery. Interest-free loans are also available from the government for small and medium sized companies for investment in energy-saving measures. There is also a UK Government scheme called Envirowise, which provides a free site visit from one of their expert advisers to identify opportunities for waste reduction/savings for companies that employ less than 250 people. These visits have come up with *savings worth thousands for companies. Think how your boss would react to a suggestion that could save them thousands of pounds annually, and the professional advice is free!*

369 Investigate if it is possible to switch to a renewable-energy supplier or to a green-energy rate in your country. Since deregulation of the electricity market in the UK, you can now choose from a wide range of companies to supply your electricity needs. This includes new companies who source 100 per cent of their supplies from renewables and traditional companies who are beginning to source some of their supplies from renewables (and who often have a special green tariff to guarantee you that 100 per cent of the supply for your business is from renewables). 1.4 million people across Europe have already signed up to green-electricity tariffs. The website www.greenprices.com has a very useful directory of companies that offer green electricity tariffs in European countries that have deregulated their markets. Green tariffs have been available from many regulated utilities in the US since the early 1990s. Following deregulation in such states as California and Pennsylvania, green rates have become increasingly available. Over 20 per cent of homes in New Hampshire and Massachusetts are now on green-energy schemes.

Sometimes this can even result in a reduction in costs. In one organisation I was involved in, when we switched to a green supplier the annual saving was over £4,000 (US$7,000 or
6,000). This was partly due to renewable energy not being subject to a climate-change levy.

370 If you have control over the lighting in your own work area, try switching the lights off if not needed during the day. *Cuts down electricity costs.*

371 Turn off any other unnecessary lights in your office. ☐
Do this only with co-operation from any others affected.
Many offices are artificially lit but could benefit from natu-
ral light, which is more relaxing to work in.

*There is an urban myth that turning off lights uses up more elec-
tricity than leaving them on. Like many such myths it once had
an element of truth. In the 1950s, fluorescent light bulbs had
a starting motor that consumed the equivalent of up to half an
hour's worth of electricity. However, that is no longer true and
all lights save electricity within approximately a minute of being
turned off.*

372 Make notebooks from scrap paper. Simply gather a ☐
bundle of sheets of paper that have been used on only one
side, cut in half and staple into a handy notepad.

Cuts waste and saves on cost of new notebooks.

373 Buy manila envelopes whenever possible. ☐

*Manila envelopes are almost invariably made from recycled
paper even if not labelled as such. They are usually the cheapest on the market – having no premium added for being made
with recycled paper.*

374 Phase out the use of letterhead printed with compa- ☐
ny executive names on it, and change to a system where
the relevant names are put in automatically by individual
computers.

*This avoids unnecessary waste when chairs, chief executives etc
change.*

375 If your letterhead is out of date, rather than dumping ☐
or recycling it, use the reverse side for internal printing or
copying.

Cuts waste, cuts costs and helps the environment.

376 If you have to keep paper copies of documents for inhouse filing, copy them on to the second side of once-used paper you no longer need. ☐

I hardly ever use virgin paper for internal record keeping at work. There is nearly always a supply of used one-sided paper around that I can use, often rescued from the recycling bin in the photocopying room. Be a little careful before reusing some papers that have had colour prints copied onto them as they might cause problems with your laser printer. Coloured paper itself can be reused with no problems.

377 Suggest that double-sided printing becomes the company standard and is the installed preference on all photo-copying machines. ☐

This can reduce your paper consumption by up to 50 per cent.

378 Email rather than use a fax machine. ☐

Faxes can involve using four sheets of paper instead of none. One sheet for your document, one for printing out at the other end, one cover sheet and one sheet to confirm activity.

379 If you have to use the fax machine, print on the back of once-used paper. ☐

380 If you have to use cover sheets for your fax machines, prepare a batch by printing or photocopying them on to the back of one-sided used paper. The same applies for any other one-sided forms for internal use. ☐

This reduces your virgin paper use without any reduction in presentation values for the organisation.

381 Switch your computer off if going for lunch and ensure the photocopiers and printers etc are all switched off before going home at night, and even more importantly at weekends. ☐

BRECSU has found that a low-energy PC used properly can be run for one sixth of the cost of a normal machine running 24 hours a day. So if there are 20 employees, that is £1,000 per year wasted and £10,000 over ten years.

382 Turn your monitor off manually when not using your ☐ PC rather than using the screen saver.

Screen savers aren't designed to be energy savers; instead they ensure that your screen doesn't get damaged by one image being burnt on to it by being left static too long. Screen savers generally only reduce electricity use by 10 watts – ie down from the 120 watts the normal cathode ray screen uses to 110 watts. Regular stand-by if activated properly uses about 30 watts, but turning the monitor off manually saves the full 120 watts.

383 Ensure that the energy-saving features of your com- ☐ puters are activated when installed.

Only 15 per cent of PCs have their energy-saving measures activated. Consult your manual or IT specialist for further help.

384 Fix a timer to vending machines, so they turn off ☐ automatically after work hours.

If your company is a nine to five operation, this would cut the annual hours of electricity use from 8,760 to 2,920. Why pay for 5,840 hours of electricity when it is of no use to anyone?

385 Provide environmental training to all those who drive ☐ company vehicles. This training should include the following:

> **386** Don't drive company vehicles above the speed ☐ limit.
>
> Fuel efficiency is best when petrol powered vehi- cles are driven between 40 to 60 mph (65 to 100 kph). Over 65 mph, you use 6 per cent extra fuel

per mile than at 60 mph, 12 per cent at 70 mph and so on.

387 Ensure air filters are not clogged.
Clogged air filters increase fuel consumption by up to 10 per cent.

388 Ensure car tyres are properly inflated.
Low pressure tyres increases fuel by up to 6 per cent.

389 Avoid rapid acceleration and braking.
This can improve fuel efficiency by between 5 and 10 per cent.

390 Ensure that vehicles are properly tuned.
Badly tuned vehicles can increase fuel use by between 10 and 20 per cent.

391 Ensure that vehicle emissions are within legal guidelines.
Fines vary from place to place, but in the UK motorists can face fines of up to £5,000 if caught with a vehicle exceeding legal pollution limits.

392 If buying a new photocopier, consider buying one of the new generation of digital photocopiers.

They are not only more efficient with paper (very simple throughput eliminates trapped paper, significantly reducing maintenance costs) but they also use less energy. Some also have instant warm up which means that they can be set to remain in the energy stand-by mode without wasting staff time.

393 Reduce the amount of computer equipment you use by linking a number of PCs together to a common printer, instead of buying an individual printer for each machine.

394 Seek staff support for using hardware a little longer than previously.

Over 2 million tonnes of electronic equipment are dumped in US landfill sites every year. In the UK, 126,000 tonnes of PC hardware is dumped each year.

395 Buy one of the new combination fax/copier/printers on the market when replacing your office equipment.

This will reduce the amount of resources used to make the products and the amount of energy spent on stand-by.

396 When buying new computer equipment, check how many years spare parts will be available after production.

If your chosen model is likely to be phased out soon, spare parts might not be available when you need to repair it, requiring you to buy a new product earlier than you would have had to otherwise.

397 Choose operating systems and software that are readily upgradable.

This will save having to throw out your entire system when upgrading, which saves on cost and reduces toxic waste. Computers whose hardware can be rewritten electronically are currently being developed; keep an eye out for their launch.

398 Buy refilled printer cartridges – if no one buys the recycled product no one will bother collecting the empty ones!

All recycling schemes need people to buy the end product as well as actually recycling them in the first place. Both refilled bubble jet and laser cartridges are available. Most companies supplying these offer a full guarantee for top quality printing.

399 If you still use them, recycled floppy discs are also available and are guaranteed 100 per cent virus and error free.

These cost significantly less than brand new discs and come with a full performance guarantee.

400 Use the stairs instead of the lift if practical. Lifts are great if you have difficulty using stairs, for moving heavy and awkward goods or if you have to go to the forty-sixth floor, but they can also institute laziness if used for just two or three floors.

Lifts are estimated to use between 5 to 15 per cent of an office block's electricity usage: the average lift uses 15,000 watts when in use. With many people having a sedentary office lifestyle, stairs are an easy exercise option and reduce electricity use. It's bizarre to see office workers paying to do exercise classes when they use the lift at work.

401 If your workplace is air-conditioned, ensure that it is only used at times of year when it is necessary.

I once worked in an office where the air-conditioning was used in winter to counteract the heating, which was too hot.

402 Try to use open windows and doors to promote natural airflow in preference to air-conditioning.

But if you are still sweltering do turn it on. Being environmentally friendly does not mean you have to be a martyr.

403 Ensure air-conditioning is only used for the area intended. In particular, keep the doors and windows closed.

Cooling air uses just as much energy as heating it and cooled air escapes in exactly the same way as hot air. If you keep your windows open the air-conditioning can use twice as much electricity – that can mean about 3 kWh of electricity wasted per average-sized room every day. With the huge peaks in electricity demand now happening in mid-summer heat waves, it is more important now more than ever that we approach air-conditioning with the same respect as heating. We don't allow the heat we have paid for to escape through wide-open windows and doors in winter, so why allow the cool air you've paid for to escape through open doors and windows in summer?

404 Set the air-conditioning thermostat at the highest temperature with which you are comfortable. This, unsurprisingly, is the opposite of what you do in winter with central heating, when you set it at the lowest temperature you are comfortable with.

Every degree the thermostat is set lower than the outside temperature in summer, costs up to 3 per cent more in electricity.

405 When installing air-conditioning units, don't put them in direct sunlight.

This forces the air-conditioning unit to work even harder unnecessarily, costing you up to 10 per cent more to run.

406 Remember to clean your air-conditioning filters regularly.

Dirty filters lead to wasted electricity, as the machine has to work harder to get the air through the filter.

407 Use glasses instead of plastic cups at the drinking fountain. If the company won't supply them, bring you own.

'Disposable' plastic cups are made from petrochemicals and are non-biodegradable, which means that for a couple of seconds of thirst quenching each day, you'll leave a mountain of plastic cups in a landfill for posterity. Each one saved will save you about 6p (11 US cents or 9 Euro cents).

408 Replace bottled water drinking fountain with a water cooler/purifier.

This saves the transporting of bottled water, eliminates waste plastic from the bottles (they can be reused for only up to a year) and removes health and safety issues connected to using *heavy bottles of water. It also saves you money – for a company of 15 people, we reduced our running costs by over £750 (US$1,400 or 1,100) per annum by changing from the bottled system to the on-site filtered water-cooler. The greater the number of staff that use the cooler, the greater the savings.*

409 Replace any old-fashioned inefficient urinals which flush every 15 minutes whether used or not, with sensor-type models or new waterless urinals.

Infrared urinals cost approximately the price of a cheap fridge each and flush only when they detect use. There are new waterless urinals on the market that don't use chemical deodorising pads. The chemical pads that the first generation of waterless urinals used have both environmental and economic costs. Both of these can dramatically reduce your water bills for such uses – depending of course on the number of male staff using the facilities. Traditional urinals can use about 23,000 UK gallons (106,000 litres or 28,000 US gallons) per year, whereas water-efficient models use about 7,000 gallons (35,000 litres or 9,100 US gallons) and waterless urinals obviously use almost no water per annum. Thus, over a ten year lifetime you can save 230,000 gallons (1,045,000 litres or 275,700 US gallons) of water by replacing just one urinal. This could save you up to £750 (US$1,300 or 1,000) per urinal.

410 Men should preferably use the urinal when they pee rather than the toilet, especially if their firm has the old-fashioned urinals that flush whether people use them or not.

This is because no extra water is involved in actually using such urinals, whereas you are probably using six to nine litres extra unnecessarily each time you use the toilet.

411 If alternative fuels are unavailable, encourage the company to purchase the most fuel-efficient vehicles or to

include this in the criteria if the company subsidises employee car purchases.

In the US, there are grants available of up to $2,000 for those buying alternatively powered vehicles. But even buying more efficient vehicles can save your company substantial amounts of money. For example, a fleet of ten new vehicles that do 30 mpg (9.4l/100 km) rather than 20 mpg (14l/100 km) will save a US company $15,000 on average over five years. British and other European drivers will save substantially more due to higher petrol prices. Simply buying a vehicle that does 25 mpg rather than 20 mpg will save an incredible 10 tonnes of CO_2 emissions over its lifetime. There are various lists analysing the environmental credentials of new cars. In the UK, these include those by the government and by the ETA (Environmental Transport Association). The number one slot in the ETA 2002 list was the Smart City Coupe 'Smart & Passion'. Remember also that the new vehicle taxation in the UK is graded on how much CO_2 emissions your car produces, so it makes financial sense also to seek out the least-polluting vehicles. Have a look at the list for your country before you decide which cars your company is going to buy.

412 Ask your company to consider phasing out company cars for those that don't really need them.

Free company cars encourage people to avoid using more benign public transport or cycling.

413 Encourage staff to use public transport instead of taxis for daytime meetings.

As well as saving your company money, this will reduce global-warming emissions from transport use by the company.

414 If many journeys by staff are local, consider a cycle pool. This is a number of cycles available for staff to use on

company business but not to take home. If you customise them with the company logo they can even act as free advertising.

An average new bicycle can cost approximately £300 (US$550 or 440). If you want a cycle that staff can fold up and take in a taxi or on public transport, they cost from approximately £300 to over £1,000 (US$1,800 or 400), but if staff regularly use taxis for short journeys, then they will pay for themselves in just 30 average taxi journeys.

415 If building a new workplace, request the architects include the most modern methods of keeping workplaces cool without the use of mechanical air-conditioning. This can be done at no extra capital cost to the building.

This can eliminate summer air-conditioning bills and capital expenditure on air-conditioning plant. This has the added bonus of reducing the threat of legionnaires disease, which has infected air-cooling systems in many countries across the globe.

416 Similarly, environmentally-aware building design can incorporate what is called passive solar design, which means that the building is built to maximise the heating potential of sunshine in winter, often at no extra cost.

Simply by building in the right shape and direction can reduce a building's heating costs by a third for its lifetime.

417 If your company is buying new furniture, suggest they save a packet by buying top class second-hand office furniture.

There are warehouses of the stuff lying around, much of it the result of companies going out of business rather than anything wrong with the furniture. Your company could even afford better quality than normal for even less. What's wrong with that?

418 Consider replacing all taps (or faucets) in workplace bathrooms with spray and push button taps.

Push button taps cost approximately the same price as a pair of jeans and save up to 50 per cent of the water used by non-push button taps. Spray attachments cost less than a half litre of wine and can be attached to taps with threaded outlets and save up to 70 per cent of the normal flow.

419 If you work at a factory, see if there is a waste exchange scheme in your area that could supply some raw materials or take some of your waste products.

By finding a market for the waste your plant produces, you not only save disposal costs but you could also find a new income stream: ie a double benefit for the profit line on your balance sheet. Finding a local source for your raw materials from another plant's waste product could also enable you to reduce raw material costs.

Suggestions that cost your company nothing

420 Ensure that empty toner and printer cartridges are recycled. Check with the cartridge supplier to see if they do this, or find out about any local charity schemes.

These cartridges are made up of a complex array of materials and involve toxic chemicals in their original manufacture. Recycling reduces the cartridge mountains left behind by our IT culture. It is estimated that 375 million are thrown away each year in the US and each one represents three quarts of oil wasted. Naturally, if you recycle your cartridge, you should also be buying re-manufactured cartridges which are often significantly cheaper than the new cartridges. The quality is nowadays is so good that they nearly all come with a full guarantee.

421 When buying new computers, see if you can choose a 'lease or takeback' option.

A number of firms such as Hewlett Packard and Dell have leasing operations and take back certain used equipment for recycling in some countries. This will soon become compulsory for all computer supply companies in the EU.

422 Check to see how much recycled plastic is used in the computer's casing.

IBM has introduced, for example, a PC with 100 per cent recycled plastic in its casing. There are now a number of environmental labelling schemes for computer equipment such as the US Energy Star, German Blue Angel, Nordic White Swan and Swiss Energy 2000. Check to see if your equipment conforms to any of these standards before buying. This reduces toxic and energy wastage.

423 When buying new computers, try to ensure that they come with the software and instruction manuals pre-installed.

This not only saves you money but also saves CDs, bulky instruction books and packaging.

424 When buying a new fax machine, ensure that it can use recycled paper and has an optional report sheet that the machine can cut into slips.

This avoids wasting an additional sheet of A4 paper to confirm activity. Alternatively, you could do away with report sheets completely.

425 Offer to carry out your own environmental audit of your firm if there is no support for spending the money on outside auditors.

You can use this book to help you to carry it out.

426 Once you have been successful in getting your company to start getting itself environmentally audited, start asking your suppliers for their environmental policies or audits.

This is how good practice can be spread down the supply chain, simply by asking the relevant questions.

427 Refuse unnecessary extra bags at the sandwich shop at lunchtime.

If a cake is already wrapped in plastic, why does it need another paper bag simply to take it back to the office?

428 Use cellulose-based adhesive tapes (eg Sellotape or Scotch tape) in preference to petrochemical-based plastic adhesive tapes.

Such tapes are made from biodegradable cellulose, usually produced from eucalyptus tree plantations and don't cost anything extra. Because they are made from trees, they will biodegrade if thrown in the compost heap, unlike the plastic based tapes which will linger for hundreds of years.

429 Introduce teleworking where appropriate for staff who have to travel long distances to work.

Travelling long distances unnecessarily and using up expensive office space for people whose work can be easily done at home does not make sense.

430 Suggest that your firm institutes a travel loan scheme for annual public transport passes.

While involving an up-front expense for the company, it is almost cost neutral over the year as the loan is repaid in full by staff. It means that they can benefit from the substantial reductions available for annual purchases.

431 If glasses are impractical for your company's drinking fountain, join a local plastic cup recycling scheme.

They will provide you with a container for the used cups and collect them for recycling, reducing your waste stream.

432 If you work in a shop, see if you can persuade your company to switch to bags made from recycled plastic or recycled paper bags.

While this may not save your company any money, it will improve its image with its customers, especially if the fact that it is a recycled bag is included with a message that your company respects the environment. These bags often cost the same or a little cheaper.

433 Check your local authority recycling website to see if there are any local schemes to take away any old unwanted computer equipment for local charities for reuse or recycling.

It is crucial that you do this, as IT equipment contains an extraordinary range of toxic materials, including: arsenic, antimony, lead, germanium, gold, aluminium, selenium, tetrabromobisphenol-A, nickel, cadmium, PVC, copper, PTFE, barium, and strontium. Between them, these materials have a wide range of toxic effects including being carcinogenic, neurotoxic (damaging to human nervous system), hormone disrupting (interfering with the normal health maintaining activities of human hormones), deadly to aquatic life or cause liver and kidney diseases in humans. I hope this evil little list will encourage you to think of others before dumping your defunct PC!

434 Get your company to switch to recycled toilet paper.

As your workplace will use far more toilet paper than your home, it is even more important to get it used there. Doing so will help create an even bigger market for the paper you recycle at home and at work. Using precious virgin paper for the toilet is simply beyond the pale.

435 It may be inappropriate to sign up with a mail preference service at work, but if you get junk mail you don't want, return it to the sender unopened with a note on the outside requesting to be removed from the mailing list. Alternatively, they often include an email address which you can use to request removal from their lists.

This has helped almost totally eliminate the deluge of mail we get in our office from recruitment and other companies.

436 Ask your company to choose a pension policy that has environmental and ethical options.

This ensures that your money is invested in companies that are environmentally responsible. It is a bit silly ensuring that your own lifestyle is saving the environment if you then help fund companies who are busily damaging it.

437 If your company feels they have to buy new furniture rather than second-hand, ensure that any wood is not from rainforest clearing.

You can get a full range of new office furniture that is certified to come only from sustainably managed woodlands. The international Forest Stewardship Council (FSC) runs such a scheme. Look out for their logo on wooden office furniture or check their website.

438 When buying calculators, ensure that you buy solar-powered rather than battery-operated calculators.

These cost no more than mains-powered calculators.

439 Instead of buying nasty plastic pens, why not buy pens made from cornstarch. It looks and feels like plastic but can rot in hours in a landfill site! Pens are also available with the body made from recycled paper.

You can buy them on the net for the same price or less than ordinary plastic pens.

440 You can also get pencils made with recycled paper instead of virgin wood.

You can buy them on the net also for the same price or less than normal pencils. These save the timber required for traditional pencils and also help provide a market for recycled paper.

441 Buy trichloroethane-free correction fluid.

Environmentally friendly correction fluid can be bought for roughly the same price as the toxic brands. Trichloroethane is an ozone-damaging chemical.

442 There is now a whole range of recycled-paper filing products on the market including box files, lever arch files, ring binders, document wallets, dividers, archive files, suspension files etc.

Buying such products expands the markets for the paper that you are hopefully now recycling.

443 Letter trays, rulers and scissors are all available made from recycled materials.

As mentioned above, buying these helps create the markets for recycled goods.

444 If your company hires catering companies for events, try hiring a vegetarian catering company, or one that has environmental credentials.

This will reduce the environmental impact from your company's catering activities.

Suggestions that cost a small amount extra

445 Suggest paper recycling at work if you are not already doing so. You can find out details on the web about recycling services available to local businesses.

There is likely to be far more paper thrown out at your workplace than at home. So if successful, you will be multiplying the positive effect you are achieving by recycling at home.

446 Suggest buying recycled photocopying paper and letterhead.

When we changed at my workplace to a recycled photocopying paper supplier, we found that we made a slight saving on the costs from our previous supplier. It also worked perfectly without any hitches on our modern photocopier. The old problems with extra dust with recycled paper are a thing of the past, with the huge improvement there has been in the quality of recycled papers. Depending on your supplier, recycled supplies of photocopying paper can be even cheaper than your current supplier.

447 Ensure that blinds are fitted to windows that receive direct sunlight.

This reduces overheating in summer and reduces air-conditioning costs. They will also reduce heat loss in winter if the premises are used at night.

448 Search the web to see if there is a special environmentally-friendly stationery supplier in your area.

There is often a small premium for these product, but these are usually such a small item on the balance sheet, that the extra expense shouldn't be significant for most companies.

449 Gently persuade your canteen or kitchen purchaser to buy organic Fair trade products such as coffee and tea.

These goods are purchased from sources that ensure that the people involved in their production in many Third World countries are paid a fair wage. They also contain no artificial chemicals.

450 Get envelope reuse labels printed with your company logo.

As well as reducing envelope consumption, these give the message to whoever you write to that your company is environmentally responsible.

451 Buy coloured markers with the body made from recycled paper.

These can be got on the net but are a bit more expensive than regular plastic markers.

452 Buy solvent-free printer labels.

These cost a bit extra, but they are worth it for the knowledge that there will be fewer solvents polluting your office. The more people buy them, the cheaper they will become.

453 If your organisation organises conferences, try and improve their environmental sustainability.

For example, you could request the environmental policies of the conference centres that you are seeking quotes from. Alternatively, you could search the web for conference venues that specialise in environmental sustainability.

Suggestions that require a significant capital investment

454 If people at your company often travel to attend meetings, consider whether having telephone conference calling or video-conferencing facilities could work instead.

Good-quality telephone conferencing machines can be got for

under £1,000 (US$1,800 or   1,400) and if staff can avoid
having to fly to meetings, it would obviously pay for itself quickly.

**455 Switch your company's vehicles to low-sulphur diesel
or Liquified Petroleum Gas (LPG).**
Diesel is more efficient than petrol, and using low-sulphur diesel
reduces pollution.

**456 The optimum fuel for cars from an environmental
point of view is actually renewable electricity.**
While electric cars reduce air-born pollution in cities, unless the
electricity is sourced renewably, it could actually be increasing
the amount of global-warming CO_2 emissions compared to
petrol-powered cars due to the emissions from power stations.
Coal-powered electricity generating stations are especially high
CO_2 polluters.

**457 Buy liquid crystal display screens when buying new
PC screens rather than the traditional bulky cathode ray
screens.**
While they are currently more expensive, as well as using far
less resources and space, they use 80 per cent less electricity
than the traditional cathode ray tube. They also don't give off
electronic emissions and have less screen flicker, both of which
benefit the user's health.

**458 Install occupancy sensors which turn lights on or off
depending on whether people are in a room.**
Many rooms in offices and factories are pointlessly left on for
hours with no one in them. I was amazed at how often people
left the lights on in the De Valois Studio at the Royal Opera
House. It is a huge studio the same size as the opera house
stage, and uses a huge bank of lights. Light sensors would significantly reduce their lighting bills.

Other suggestions

1 _____ ☐

2 _____ ☐

3 _____ ☐

4 _____ ☐

5 _____ ☐

_____

	Year 1	Year 2	Year 3	Year 4	Year 5
Suggestions Score (subtotal)					

Chapter 9
Out and About

Work aside, there is a whole host of ways in which our habits when we are out and about in the world can damage or protect the environment. Many of us are members of organisations of one sort or another, whether it is a charity or sports association, an old people's club or pressure group. We are also all customers of a large range of companies, from local shops and supermarkets to banks and travel agencies. All these organisations consume resources and will usually have a far larger environmental footprint than you will in your own home. By gently requesting them to take environmental considerations into account in how they are run, you can have an influence on thousands of people.

Whether it is the pesticide policy we got my local council to adopt, the environmental audit carried out by the charity I am a director of or the fact that my national membership organisation's HQ now only uses recycled photocopying paper, I know that the impact of my efforts 'out and about' multiplies what I am doing in my own home many thousand fold. Take recycled paper, for example. I use less than 500 sheets at home a year and nearly all of that is reused paper. The HQ uses over 2 million sheets every year. Since they changed their policy seven years ago, my success in transferring my own practice at home to the HQ has now resulted in 14 million sheets of recycled paper instead of virgin paper being bought.

That is the sort of positive power that you can have in the wider world if armed with having sorted out your own home's

environmental performance. Once you have started using recycled paper at home, consider writing to your bank and asking
them why they aren't using recycled paper or raise it at the
AGM of your charity or bowling club. Ask them to start auditing their environmental performance, no matter who they are.
Get the football club to audit their water use and see if they
can get their bills reduced by simple measures such as press-
button showers or spray taps. The list of things you can take
up in the wider world is endless. Choose one and see what
happens. It really is very rewarding to see positive change taking place as a result of your actions.

Remember, try to be gentle. There is no need to feel frus-
trated if you don't succeed at your first attempt. It is normal
for it to take some time for people and organisations to appreciate the need for the environmental changes that you already
feel strongly about. But the lesson I would like to pass on is
that persistence and working with other people nearly always
pays off. If you don't get a satisfactory letter back from the bank
or your question is sidelined at the AGM, find other reasonable ways to raise it. Find out who the key decision-makers
are and approach them. Seek out other like-minded people and
work together. Don't forget to acknowledge your victories
large or small, whether it's getting your local tenants association to switch from Nescafe to fair trade tea or when your
bank writes back and says it will change to recycled paper in
the future. Each and every step is important.

Outside the home, over 20 per cent of greenhouse gas
emissions are emitted by transport vehicles. Transport is
expected to be the largest source of emissions by 2020 if
current trends continue, with aeroplanes one of the fastest-
expanding sources of greenhouse gases. Worldwide there are
now 776 million vehicles in use, with 223 million of these in
the United States alone. As prices drop, millions more people
in the developing world are now naturally acquiring cars. The

trend towards ever larger cars including people carriers and four-wheel drives continues unabated in many developed countries such as the US and UK. In the UK there are now over 32 million vehicles on the road network. That equates to 60 million tonnes of raw materials in the cars and 900,000 million litres (234 billion US gallons) of petrol every year. The cost in environmental damage caused by them is estimated by the UK Government to be over 52 billion pounds.

There is of course also a deep human as well as environmental price for car use. WHO worldwide figures reveal that a person dies from a road crash every minute of every day. That equates to 1,440 people every day or over half a million people every year. Over 3,000 people die on UK roads alone each year. That is over 60 times the number of UK soldiers who were killed in the latest invasion of Iraq. The WHO estimates that even more people – three million, in fact – die each year from air pollution, much of which comes from vehicle emissions. The Lancet reported in 2000 that in France, Austria and Switzerland, over 20,000 deaths each year could be attributed directly to pollution from vehicle emissions. This is because vehicles emit toxic chemicals as well as greenhouse gases. These toxic chemicals include benzene, which is carcinogenic; hydrocarbons which cause the photochemical smog that worsens asthma; nitrogen oxides which cause asthma and bronchitis and acid rain when the chemical mixes with clouds; and carbon monoxide which can damage the nervous system and is also a contributor to global warming.

Asthma is on the increase worldwide with over 100 million people with the condition and over 180,000 people dying from it every year. For example, levels in Switzerland and the UK have increased fourfold in the last 30 years, and they are up over 60 per cent in the US since the 1960s. Research has shown a direct link between vehicle pollution and increased incidences of attacks for asthma sufferers.

I was shocked when I became involved in my local community to discover that the number of kids in local schools suffering from chronic asthma had risen astronomically. Local teachers told me that it is now normal for a row of asthma respirators to sit on a shelf in nearly all classes. One teacher said this was a phenomenal change from when she started teaching locally, when chronic asthma was almost unheard of. While cycling around the borough, I had noticed that the council's own vehicles, such as garbage trucks and school buses, were among the worst polluters on the streets. I contacted the local paper suggesting that the council should test their own vehicle emissions. One of the council's senior officers read the article and set out to do something about it. This resulted in the council joining an ingenious initiative to pool the buying power of councils across Europe to bring down the price of cleaner municipal vehicles. My local council ended up with one of the largest cleaner vehicle fleets in the UK by switching to natural gas and electric propelled vehicles.

Having successfully got our local council to switch to cleaner vehicles I decided to see if we could be equally successful in closing a road that sliced through my local green-space, Burgess Park. It was used by many drivers as a shortcut on their way to work, causing a horrendous amount of noise and pollution. If at all possible, roads should not cut through parks. There should be areas of natural beauty where children and adults can escape from the built environment, and walk and play without the fear of being run over or being stressed by noise and pollution.

As I cycled past the road slicing through the park each day I would imagine the road closed. Working with the support of a large number of parents who were worried about the threat to their children's safety and other local amenity groups, we persuaded the council officers to consider our proposals to close the road. Significantly, a footpath leading to a school crossed the road at a sharp corner within the park, which had been the site of many crashes. The officers prepared a number of options for the council's Traffic Committee, which then voted in favour of closure! Two years later the road closed permanently and I was delighted. This formerly little used area of the park is now heavily made use of by local kids and parents as the danger, noise and pollution from cars is no more.

I really enjoyed becoming a cyclist again when I stopped dancing professionally and was pleasantly surprised at how fast I could get around the city. Journeys that I allowed an hour for on public transport would now take only 25 minutes and of course I generally had no problems finding parking wherever I went. I now cycle to work each day and love the convenience and dependability. In summer the breeze you get while cycling is far more comfortable than putting up with the furnace-like heat on the underground. I have taken the view that as I don't have the expense of running a car, I should invest in good-quality raingear. The only problem I find is ice. Black ice is as much a hazard for cyclists as it is for car drivers, so I treat icy weather with a lot of respect.

Cycling saves me quite a considerable amount of money each year and as I only work part time this is really welcome. According to the London Assembly, cycling is healthier, cheaper and quicker than any other form of transport in London. The British Medical Association also back cycling as a good way to achieve physical fitness and as an excellent means of reducing susceptibility to heart disease. Indeed research quoted by the WHO found that even after adjustment to include leisure time activity, those that did not cycle to work experienced a 39 per cent higher mortality rate than those who did. Cyclists have fewer colds and lower stress levels than the ordinary population.

I am always on the lookout for ways to improve things for pedestrians and cyclists in my neighbourhood. We again successfully persuaded our local council to require automatic cycle-parking provisions for all new commercial and residential apartment-block developments. They are required to be both easily accessible for cyclists and genuinely secure. Putting in cycle racks in a dark, hard to find car park is not much use to anyone. I am now working on getting the town planners to take cycle storage into account when building new individual domestic houses. How often have you seen people lugging cycles through a house to put them out the back, dirtying the walls and carpets en route, or seen bikes clogging up the hallways and entrances to peoples homes, making them look scruffy? One solution is to require the architects to design a space inside the front door that would be suitable for cycle and pram (or stroller) parking. I have submitted such proposals for the latest review of the council's planning guidance and at a recent meeting to discuss it they were positive – so watch this space!

Many of the ways we can improve our home's environmental sustainability also apply to us while on holiday. The water, resource, waste, energy and transport issues are again all relevant whether you are on a touring holiday in Scotland or a sun and sand break in Torremolinos.

Ideally, I would love to see an international aviation tax, which could fund the constructive work the United Nations is doing in, for example, famine relief, conflict resolution and the elimination of infectious diseases. However, I think this will take a little longer to achieve than the closure of our local shortcut! If you do have to take a long-distance journey, you should always check to see if there is a train alternative. If you take into account the time necessary for travelling to and from the airports and for checking in, some high-speed train links can be faster than plane journeys. Trains use less than a quarter of the energy used by planes per passenger/kilometre.

It would not be realistic to suggest that no one flies until we have found a way of doing so that does not contribute to climate change, but one constructive thing we all can do as well as cutting down our number of flights is to ensure that we plant a tree for every flight that we take. As it grows up, this tree will soak up some of the CO_2 that your journey emitted. There are even some travel companies who will do this for you. I am lucky in that I have already quite a substantial CO_2 bank balance through the community planting that I organised in my local park. This winter the council had a scheme asking residents for suggestions for locations for new street trees. As the street opposite from where I live has an industrial estate near by, I thought it would be great to have a row of trees that would improve the view out people's front doors (as well as help trap some of the pollutants that the traffic emitted.) I was delighted to come home a few weeks ago to find that my suggestion had been taken up and I am looking forward to seeing them mature over the coming years.

I love to go on holidays to yoga and meditation centres in Greece or Spain. They usually offer vegetarian food and buy much of their food locally, which reduces the food miles and packaging involved (not to mention being delicious). They all have wonderful walks and swimming nearby, so there is no need to hire a car or be constantly travelling. I invariably buy a bottle of water on my first day away and from then on fill it from the tap. The water in the yoga centre I go to in Greece is fed by a mountain spring and is delicious, so what's the point of wasting money on bottled water and leaving a mountain of empty plastic bottles behind me when I return to London?

What is true for holidays is also true when we are out and about near home, even if it is only a trip to the cinema. Realising that you are always responsible for your environmental footprint is again the name of the game. How you use energy, resources, water or transport is still always relevant. Just because you are just on a trip into town, does not mean that you should not care about the environmental consequences of your actions. I avoid fast-food joints when in town due to their appalling throwaway culture and I also try to ensure if I am going for coffee it is a place that provides proper mugs rather than paper ones. Americans spend over $120 billion on fast food every year and the Missouri Department of Transport estimates that a third of litter comes from fast-food outlets. The millions of disposed styrofoam burger cartons take over a million years to decompose in landfill sites, while a paper bag takes only a month.

I also carry a spoon in my rucksack in case there are only disposable spoons available for stirring my coffee. I will often order a jug of table water rather than bottled water when in restaurants and will refuse excessive paper napkins whether in a restaurant or takeaway. I also usually cycle in, which means that I can get home in double quick time afterwards.

While pleased with the changes I have helped achieve in many of the organisations I have been involved in, I always have daydreams of trying to manage even more campaigns. I would like to get supermarkets to stock more environmentally sustainable goods, get my bank to start environmental auditing or to get my gas company to use recycled paper for their communications. I hope you will have the time to be able to take up some of these issues, as well as take on board some of the suggestions below for your own exploits out in the wider world outside your home. Even if you have never done anything like this before, you will soon be able to report your own stories of success.

How to score

3   if you do the suggestion nearly all the time

2   if you do it occasionally or fairly often

1   if you hardly ever do it

0   if you never do it

Suggestions that save money

459 Do not use your car to go the couple of hundred metres down the road for a bottle of milk.

Over a third of car journeys are less than two miles (3.2 km), which are perfect for cycling or walking. A bicycle is one of the cheapest modes of transport. By cycling to work, I save the price of a new washing machine every year, as well as keeping myself fit.

460 If you have to use your car to travel to work, set up a car-sharing arrangement with other people undertaking the same journey.

This not only saves between 50 and 75 per cent of petrol costs and reduces maintenance costs, but it also reduces the amount of emissions per person per journey and also reduces traffic congestion. Check the web to see if there is a car-sharing scheme near you.

461 If you drive your kids to school, see if there is a walking or cycling 'bus scheme' in your area. If there isn't, encourage your school to set one up.

This is where trained parents collect kids from various homes and walk or cycle them safely to school on a rota instead of using a number of polluting and congestion-causing vehicles.

462 Drive more efficiently.

A car at 50 mph uses 30 per cent less fuel than a car going at 70 mph. That is a significant saving in petrol costs per long journey. Poignantly, 45 per cent of pedestrians hit by cars travelling at 30 mph are killed, whereas it is only 5 per cent with cars travelling at 20 mph.

463 Turn your car engine off if you are stopping for a minute or longer.

Saves petrol and stops polluting the local street where you are stopped.

464 Instead of shopping by car, get baskets put on the front and rear of your bicycle and you will be amazed how much you can carry with very little effort.

Saves the cost of petrol and parking, reduces local pollution, traffic congestion and danger to local kids from traffic. It helps keep you fit as well at no extra charge.

465 Walk, cycle or use public transport when on holiday.

You will be able to appreciate the area's beauty far more this way than if you are whizzing by in a car, and you are more likely to meet local people. Some travel companies specialise in cycling or walking holidays, which eliminate car hire and petrol costs as well as reducing pollution. I often go on holiday to places where there are no or very few cars. This helps me to relax more and of course means I have no extra travel expenses while there.

466 Order soda water rather than bottled mineral water in pubs. Mineral water comes in bottles that are not returnable in many countries.

Many places won't charge you for soda water, so it saves your pocket as well as reducing the waste-glass mountain.

467 Avoid designer beer bottles in pubs that are obviously not returnable. Order tap beer instead.

Beer kegs are the most efficient method of transporting beers or lagers and avoiding all packaging waste. Draught beer is also usually cheaper and is more environmentally friendly to transport due to far lower bulk.

468 In restaurants, order a jug of tap water in preference to bottled water.

It reduces the bill and avoids a trail of wasted water bottles in your wake.

469 If on holiday in a hot country where the tap water is drinkable, buy a glass water bottle with a screw top on the first day and then refill it each day. Alternatively, you could buy a hiker's insulated bottle, which keeps water cool, to take with you. Of course, the same applies if you use bottled water while out and about at home.

This could save you buying up to twenty bottles of water unnecessarily while on holiday and, if everyone did it, it would reduce by up to a factor of almost twenty the billions of plastic bottles left after our holidays, in beautiful resorts across our planet.

470 Check the web and see if there is a green-currency scheme in your neighbourhood. These are often known by names such as LETS or time banks. They are a means for people to trade with each other without using money but still allowing choice.

They are good for the environment as they encourage people to trade locally, thus avoiding polluting transport. They also encourage people to get things repaired that they may not have otherwise.

Suggestions that cost nothing

471 If going on holiday, use travel companies that provide environmentally friendlier holidays. They are easy to find on the web.

These companies specialise in trips that try to reduce the environmental impact of tourism.

472 When staying in a hotel, use towels sensibly. The fact that there are four towels in a room doesn't mean that you need to use four towels every day! Many hotels now have a system where they only wash towels left on the floor. Make sure you use this system wisely, and if the hotel doesn't have the system, suggest it to them.

Washing towels uses up a large amount of water, heat and detergent, so wasting this on clean towels just does not make sense.

473 If buying souvenirs or presents on holiday, try to buy items made locally.

This reduces transport mileage and creates a market for locally-produced materials.

474 Dispose of plastic beer-can-holders safely.

Too many birds and wildlife lose their lives from getting entangled in these plastic rings.

475 Don't allow helium balloons to blow away.

They can become a menace to wildlife and can even suffocate them.

476 If you have to have a car and want an emergency breakdown service, consider joining a driving association that is not part of the transport lobby, such as the Environmental Transport Association (ETA) in the UK or the Better World Club in the US.

The ETA provides a similar national breakdown service to the other automobile associations but doesn't use your membership fee to lobby government on behalf of the road lobby. Instead, they lobby to reduce car use and to increase sustainable alternatives to car use. They claim their average call-out time is 35 minutes and they fix over 80 per cent of breakdowns at the roadside. The large mainstream automobile clubs that provide emergency breakdown cover in the US similarly use their members' money to lobby against many environmental initiatives, such as the Cleaner Air Act. The Better World Club also provides an emergency breakdown service, but will not use your money to do such disastrous lobbying in your name.

477 Never, ever pour used motor oil down the drain!
A tiny amount of oil can pollute an immense amount of water. Check with your local council about their oil disposal service. Recycled oil is now used for central heating.

478 If visiting friends for a dinner party or a party where you bring your own bottle, bring an organic wine.
Organic wines are now readily available in supermarkets and are often no more expensive than regular wines. A wider range can be found by shopping on the internet. Buying organic wine means that you reduce pesticide use in vineyards. Some people claim that they have less severe hangovers from organic wine – but I think this depends more on how many bottles you consume.

479 If visiting a major tourist attraction, return the guide to the entrance when you are finished.
Major tourist attractions like the Statue of Liberty or Westminster Abbey receive millions of visitors each year. This currently means millions of brochures are thrown away needlessly, when they could easily be reused.

480 In cafes etc, don't use disposable teaspoons. Keep a reusable spoon in your bag for use when out and about.

Like saving your pennies, every little bit of waste reduction counts.

481 If you have to use a fast-food restaurant or takeaway, don't accept more napkins, sugar sachets, condiments or creamers than you actually need. Just hand them back politely and say thanks but you don't need them.

Most fast-food outlets give almost every customer more items than they need, which then get dumped unused, adding unnecessarily to their already huge waste mountain.

482 Even if you aren't vegetarian, consider visiting a vegetarian restaurant for a change once in a while. You may be surprised at the tasty foods that are available. Alternatively you could consider ordering the vegetarian option occasionally in non-vegetarian restaurants.

Every meat-free meal that you consume reduces the huge amount of resources poured into meat production. They are usually cheaper than meat-based restaurants too. People in many non-vegetarian societies have meat only once a week.

483 For an extra treat you could go even further and go to a restaurant that specialises in serving organic food.

Frequenting such restaurants helps to build the momentum to put an end to chemical-based factory farming.

484 If you are picnicking in the countryside or while on holiday, ensure that you dispose of any waste responsibly. You can bury any organic waste and take back recyclables and other waste for responsible disposal.

Rubbish irresponsibly left in the countryside is not only unsightly but poses a danger to human safety and to the wildlife that live there.

485 If you are the last person leaving a room, such as a public bathroom or a training studio, ensure you turn the lights off. Just don't leave anyone on the toilet in total darkness or turn lights off that are needed for safety reasons. ☐

It really astounds me how many people do not feel empowered enough to turn off lights when out of their home. They feel they have the right to turn lights on but very rarely to turn them off. It seems to be always 'someone else's' responsibility.

486 Ask any community organisations or clubs you are a member of to consider having an environmental audit. ☐

This will really give them the starting tools to sort out their environmental performance and will even identify a number of measures that will save them money.

487 Alternatively, get them to start with a simple water use or energy audit. ☐

There are often many low-cost options that can save money quickly on many club premises. See the list of suggestions in the water and work chapters, many of which will apply to club premises as much as your home or office. Grants are often available for water and energy improvements to community or voluntary groups. Check with your local energy or water information services.

488 If you are a member of a charity or local community group, ask them if they have an environmental purchasing policy. If they don't, ask them to consider initiating one. A sample purchasing policy would be: ☐

This organisation XXXXX recognises that the purchasing decisions of our employees/officers can make a positive contribution to environmental sustainability. We therefore commit ourselves to the purchase of recycled and environmentally preferable products wherever practicable. 'Environmentally preferable products' means products that do less damage to the environment and human health when compared with competing products. This comparison may consider raw materials sourcing, production, packaging, distribution, reuse, operation, maintenance, energy use, recyclability or disposal of the product. 'Practicable' means sufficient in performance and available at a reasonable price.

This will help reform your organisation's purchasing habits and make a real difference.

489 Ask any groups with which you are associated in the community if they use recycled paper for their photocopying/ publications and if not, ask them to consider doing so. Do your own research yourself into the local suppliers and costs, which often can easily be done on the web – this may make them more open to listening to your idea.

This will help create a market for the paper you recycle.

490 If you are a director of a charity, community group etc, ask your board to formally pass a motion requiring that the annual accounts include an environmental audit of the organisation's activities.

An environmental audit is one of the quickest ways to transform your environmental performance.

491 If your utility company, bank or pension company does not use recycled paper for its communications with you, write to them the next time they send you a bill and ask them why not. You could go one further and ask them do they have an annual environmental audit and, if not, why not?

Asking a simple question can release the power of action for positive change.

492 Ensure that you bank with a company that does not invest in companies that destroy the environment.

Saving the planet at home while funding the companies that destroy it through your bank account does not make sense.

493 When buying a house, choose a mortgage company that does not invest in environmentally damaging projects.

When choosing a mortgage company for my own home, I chose a mutual building society, as I knew that they would not invest the profits from my mortgage in environmentally damaging industries or the arms trade but in helping others to buy their own home.

494 Include an environmental charity in your will.

All our lives involve environmental costs no matter how environmentally responsible we are, and including such a charity in our wills is an excellent way of making a contribution to the next generation in recognition of this.

495 If you have spare cash to invest in stocks and shares, invest it in environmentally benign companies or, even better, companies that are actively investing in methods to save the planet such as responsible wind energy or organic food companies.

There is now also a large range of ethical investment portfolios that you can choose to invest your money in.

Suggestions that cost a small amount extra

496 If you are too busy to campaign for a better environment, why not join Friends of the Earth, Greenpeace or WWF?

They will use your membership to pay for people to lobby governments and businesses on your behalf. The funds they have available for such lobbying are a fraction of what the big corporations with their vested interests have at their disposal. You can help achieve a better balance, all for a small annual direct debit. You also get a regular members newsletter which helps keep you up to date with the latest environmental issues.

497 If you do have to travel by plane, consider planting or paying for the planting of a tree for each journey you take.

There are now travel companies that will do this automatically for you if you book through them. The new trees will help lock up the CO_2 released by your journey. Every 1000 km (621 miles) flown emits approximately 250 kg (550 lb) of CO_2 per person.

498 Avoid cafes, restaurants and fast-food outlets that use disposable cutlery and plates.

The alternatives may be a little more expensive but such fast-food outlets are the most visible expression of our disposable society, and lead to literally mountains of waste dumped every year with all the pollution, destruction of natural habitats and global-warming emissions that involves.

499 Join a major political party (whoever is closest to your own values) and becomes part of their internal environmental pressure group seeking to make the environment central to what its party stands for. Democracy only works if those seeking positive change participate in the decision-making processes.

Minimum membership subscriptions often start for as little as the price of a bottle of wine. Check on the web for rates. Special rates usually apply for students and the unemployed. So many people condemn politicians for all the planet's woes, yet political parties are simply collections of ordinary people like you and me. Being part of the solution rather than simply complaining is so much more empowering.

500 Use a mosquito net rather than electric mosquito killers
that emit chemical fumes for protection, when on holiday.

*A mosquito net costs about the equivalent of two bottles of wine
but will last you for life if you take care of it. It will save you
the cost of buying chemical mosquito coils or tablets for the electric mosquito killers.*

501 If you have a car, get it serviced regularly.

*This ensures that it works at its maximum efficiency and that it
isn't emitting excessive pollution. This will reduce petrol consumption and so save you money.*

502 Don't drive with your windows open unnecessarily
and don't drive around with heavy objects in the back of
the car that you do not use.

*Both increase the amount of petrol required to power the car
and so eliminating them will save you money wasted on petrol.*

Suggestions that require a significant capital investment

503 If you have an old car from the days before catalytic
converters were compulsory, get one installed.

*Once warmed up, catalytic converters significantly reduce the
emissions of many of your vehicle's pollutants such as carbon
monoxide and hydrocarbons by up to 90 per cent and nitrous
oxides by up to 70 per cent. They cost the equivalent of two pairs
of jeans plus installation depending on the make of your car.*

504 Buy a bicycle if you haven't got one and are able to
cycle. Also purchase bikes for your kids. Get them trained
in road safety before letting them on the roads.

*The bicycle is one of the most efficient machines invented by
humanity. It is the most effective form of pollution-free local*

transport and is a great way of maintaining fitness. Introducing kids to cycling at a young age is one of the most effective ways of enabling them to have the cycling habit all of their lives. Many adults have a resistance to cycling if they haven't learnt as children.

505 If you have trouble cycling, consider buying an electric bicycle.

They are now much lighter with some models weighing as little as 45 lb (20 kg). The 200 W motor can go for up to 15 miles (24.2 km) at 15 mph, (24.2 kmph) on a 3 hour electric charge (ensure it is from a renewable supplier!). They can also be set to only kick in when you really need the extra help, such as when going up hills. They cost about £870 each (US$1,600 or 1,300).

506 If your car runs on petrol, investigate the feasibility of switching to alternative fuels such a LPG (Liquefied Petroleum Gas) which emit less global warming CO_2 per mile. Many motor manufacturers now offer dual use vehicles, which can run on either LPG or petrol, so that you need not fear being unable to find an LPG station.

A dual-use kit costs about £550 + installation (US$1,000 or 800). They emit lower levels of particulates, CO_2, No_2, Hydrocarbons and CO. One fill of the gas will last about 260 miles (419 km) depending on the size of your car. It costs half the price of diesel or petrol per litre.

507 If you are unable to cycle, consider buying an electric car for local journeys, but only if you have chosen to change to a renewable electricity supplier through your mains or if you produce your own renewable electricity in quantities large enough.

The current commercially-available electric cars do about 3.7 m/kWh (6 km/kWh) of electricity. They need to be recharged every 100 miles (161 km) and so are ideal for regular journeys such as going to work and back. They have a top speed of 78 mph (125 kmph).

508 When buying a new car, ensure that it is the most efficient in its class

Fuel efficiency for similar-sized cars can vary between different makes by as much as 45 per cent. This will not only ensure that you reduce your CO_2 emissions by up to 45 per cent for the lifetime of your car but it can also reduce your fuel costs by up to the same amount. Forty-five per cent of the money you spend every year on fuel is really worth thinking about. Wouldn't you rather spend the money on something more fun than petrol? The gas/electric hybrid Honda Insight was found to be the US's most fuel-efficient car in 2003 with 66 mpg (4.28 l/100 km). The electricity comes from capturing the energy formerly wasted from the brakes.

Other suggestions

1 _____

_____

2 _____

_____

3 _____

_____

4 _____

_____

5 _____

_____

	Year 1	Year 2	Year 3	Year 4	Year 5
Suggestions Score (subtotal)					

Chapter 10
From Med School to Environmental Activist
(via the Ballet Stage!)

Many people ask how I became an environmentalist, and sometimes I too look back perplexed at how I jumped from medical student to professional classical dancer to passionate political campaigner on behalf of our threatened environment and the deputy chair of one of Britain's major political parties!

After leaving school in 1979, I went to the National University of Ireland in Cork, where I indulged my fascination with human anatomy and spent four years studying medicine. However, I spent two of my summer vacations in the United States, where I was introduced to the then new theories of how human emotions and psychology could affect one's physiology and so create disease. I came back to my university full of enthusiasm for these new ideas and hit my conservative professors like a tomato fired at a blank wall. I soon decided that Western medicine was no longer my preferred career path and abandoned med school.

Attending a party soon after, I met a dancer from the local amateur ballet company Cork City Ballet. I asked my new friend where someone my age could try a ballet class. She suggested I try the Cork Ballet School and so started a new passion that was to teach me a very important lesson for my later environmental activism. That lesson was that with a single-minded determination, the seemingly impossible can be made to happen. The standard belief is that it is impossible to become a professional dancer if starting at 21 years of age. I not only wanted to become a professional dancer but had a dream of dancing at the Royal Opera House at Covent Garden.

I actually succeeded in becoming a fully-paid-up professional dancer within two years, when I got a contract with the Dublin City Ballet. Then just six years later, I was standing with over 500 other dancers auditioning to dance with the Royal Opera in their new production of Wagner's *Tannhauser*. They first divided us into two groups of 250. They then whittled us down to two groups of one hundred and then groups of 20. Those of us who were then left had to dance across the huge De Valois studio one by one. I survived each elimination stage with growing nervousness and disbelief. My excitement knew no bounds when I was told that I had been selected as one of the 18 lucky dancers for the production. I had been working part time in the restaurant Maxim's de Paris as a waiter and after the audition, in true cliché fashion, I leaped my way in the rain down Longacre to work, deliriously happy. My dream of dancing on the Covent Garden stage had come true!

For ten years ballet was all-consuming for me. I ate, drank and slept ballet. I gave little thought to what else went on in the wider world. I had no awareness of the environmental crises facing our planet, but that was to change dramatically.

While dancing I maintained my physical and emotional health by regular sessions with an acupuncturist, Andrea Durant, and a homeopath/therapist, Linda Mutch. One day Linda mentioned that she and her partner Brian were going on a trip with a group of alternative medical practitioners to the heart of the Amazon rainforest, to try to meet the Yanomami Indians who lived there. They were the only group that year to receive permission to visit the Yanomami from the Venezuelan government. Linda said that there was a vacancy in the group as one person had dropped out. I had a little bit of spare cash as my father had recently died and left me some money, so I bit my finger and said yes there and then to going. This spur of the moment decision would change my life completely.

On the month-long trip, I ended up separating from Linda's group and spent over two weeks by myself with a group of Yanomami Indians in the heart of the Amazonian rainforest. It was a truly amazing experience and privilege to share that time with these people. Their ancestors have lived in this region for over 20,000 years and their lifestyle has left no legacy of environmental destruction behind them during all that time. One thus has to question many of the presumptions underlying our 'civilisation'. I am convinced that we have to learn lessons from these people if our own civilisation is to be diverted from its headlong rush to destroy the very environment on this planet that provides it with a home and nourishment.

That said, I could not help but feel that the future was bleak for the Yanomami. While their lifestyle was stunning in its respect for nature (and they were wonderful hosts to me), they had no concept of ownership of the land on which that teeming rainforest thrived. Of the over 6 million indigenous people living in the Amazonian region when Europeans first arrived in the early 17th century, there are today less than 600,000 left. The Yanomami were first encountered by Europeans only in the 1950s, and they are already threatened with extinction by miners, roads, American fundamentalist Christian missionaries and our deadly Western diseases.

I was profoundly upset by my feeling that these people were mortally endangered by the continuing encroachment by the West. I resolved that when I returned to Britain I would do my best to change my consumerist lifestyle. The destruction of the rainforest is a by-product of how we live. No matter how much effort goes into protecting the rainforest, if we don't deal with our destructive consumption habits, then the forests will eventually perish anyway and their people with them. At the end of my time with the Yanomami they held a ceremony and made me an honorary shaman of their tribe. I still have the head-dress and armbands to this day. While I gently turned down their invitation to join their tribe, they indicated that they did not wish other non-Yanomami to come to them. They are rightly very protective of their culture and independence.

When I returned to England I continued as a freelance ballet dancer, mainly working on various contracts at the Royal Opera House. I started to do little things like taking my glass bottles to the recycling bank and resolving to buy at least one piece of organic food each time I went to the supermarket. Then one day a leaflet dropped through my door that was to prove to be the next crucial step in my initiation into environmental activism and politics. It was a circular from the local council regarding a proposed regeneration scheme for my area. I lived on the border between Camberwell and Peckham in London, in an area that was made up of massive tower blocks built in the 1970s and early 1980s. Five of the reputedly worst housing estates in Britain were then within a ten minute walk of my home.

The main break from this densely-built environment was the large Burgess Park, which had been gradually created since World War II. It had been assembled from a series of old bombsites, by the compulsory purchase of industrial buildings along the old Surrey Canal and through the purchase and subsequent demolition of a maze of Victorian terraced housing. Indeed many of my neighbours had been moved out of these homes with the promise of a better life in the new tower blocks with the park as their new green lung.

I walked through the park every day on my way to the bus stop and had grown to like it. Part of my route went past one of the few sections that been landscaped. It had a large sign stating it was a designated wildlife site, and had a meadow and a significant number of maturing trees. When I looked at the brochure that had come through my door, for some reason I noticed that the wildlife site was coloured white while the rest of the park was green. I checked in my A–Z street map and saw that the wildlife site was coloured green there. I started making inquiries and found that the council was indeed proposing to sell this wildlife site to a developer.

Having forced people out of their homes and into disastrous tower blocks to create the park, they were now proposing to sell the cleared parkland to help pay for the refurbishment of the disastrous blocks. Local people had paid too high a price for their promised park for it to be squandered just as it was becoming mature. I investigated further and to my horror found out that the council was proposing to remove the open space protection for the rest of the park. So, not having a clue how to go about it, I became an activist.

I had no real understanding then of how the political decision-making process worked. I phoned and wrote to everyone I could think of and attended the local Environmental Forum, where I found a wealth of local activists from all the local environmental groups. This included the then chair Danielle Byrne who shortly after was to become the national chair of Friends of the Earth. She was a wealth of knowledge about the local scene and an invaluable ally in my new campaign.

Through all these good people my awareness of global environmental problems expanded. I became aware of how almost all of our precious natural inheritance was under attack from our new, devastating lifestyle. Our water was under threat from the pesticides and chemicals we used indiscriminately. Our air was under threat from the pollutants that poured out of our vehicles, power stations and factories. Our soil was under threat from factory farming, with millions of tonnes annually lost worldwide from soil erosion. Our wild animals and plants were being lost at an ever-increasing rate due to our own population explosion and the destruction of natural habitats. Even the precious gift of sunshine was becoming a potential source of cancer due to the loss of the ozone layer.

The threat to our very genetic inheritance posed by GM foods and animals I was only to learn about later. This awareness of how destructive our lifestyles had become was the bequest of the 1980s environmentalists. The challenge for the activists of the 1990s was to identify remedies and to start campaigning for their implementation. The challenge now that the new century has started is to mainstream many of these solutions.

As I began working to protect the park, I was rehearsing for Saint-Saen's *Samson & Delilah* which had Placido Domingo singing the role of Samson. I was selected to partner, with three other male dancers, the Royal Ballet's principal ballerina Deborah Bull, who was guesting with the Opera Ballet in the wild bacchanalean ballet with which the opera spectacularly ends. The choreography was by David Bintley. I was really excited about it and it was one of the pieces that I most enjoyed performing in during my career. For some bizarre reason I had fancied dancing in a loincloth on the Royal Opera stage and I had got my wish! Little did I know that it was to be my last professional engagement.

By the time I had completed my final performance in Samson, my campaign to save the park had completely taken over my life. I still had some money left in my bank account from my fathers will – I decided not to look for another dance contract and use this money to devote myself full time to saving the park. On paper this was a crazy decision and totally out of keeping with my previous all-consuming obsession with ballet. However, gradually, and without in the least suspecting it, another passion had crept in and claimed a place in my heart. I had leapt from the ballet stage to the environmental and political stage.

In the end I spent nearly an entire year off work. My time was spent going to meetings, collecting petitions, revitalising a local action group, lobbying politicians, staging demonstrations and talking to the local press. I bought a computer, which as a dancer I didn't even know how to turn on, but with the help of my then boyfriend Robert Hacking, it soon became an essential tool in my campaign. The Liberal Democrat councillors, who were the opposition on the local council, were helpful. The 1992 British general election was coming up. They appeared to me to be environmentally the best major political party in British politics. I had always admired the proportional electoral system that I had grown up with in Ireland and they were also campaigning for this to be introduced into Britain, so I decided to stop sitting on the sidelines and signed up.

Again, little did I realise that liberal politics would come to take another central role in my life. While I continued my campaigning on the park, I quickly became involved in local politics and soon was selected as a candidate for the 1994 council elections in a target ward that had been held for generations by the Labour Party. We campaigned on halting the blanket spraying of pesticides on council estates, against the sell off and destruction of the park and reducing crime. With the help of my colleagues Alf Langley and Ruth Clark (who is an amazing one-person electoral machine) we achieved a miracle and won! Within two years I had gone from being a full-time professional ballet dancer to being an elected politician. I admit to being a bit overwhelmed by the speed of the change.

An additional miracle was that, after all my campaigning, I ended up on the very council committee that was considering the park-land sales and its planning status. I was able to successfully propose that we drop the land sales and restore the open-space protection for the entire park. All the hard work and time campaigning had paid off fantastically!

But the park continued to be under threat. During the following decade I was to lead over 44 different campaigns against various developers and council officers who always eyed this piece of inner-London real estate with greedy eyes. We fought off nearly everything you could imagine, including proposals for industrial estates, housing estates, a five-acre indoor leisure complex, a secondary school, bus routes and new roads. We won almost every one of these fights mainly because we won the original battle to retain the open space protection in the borough plan. We are now negotiating with the local community and council to see if we can protect the park in perpetuity by placing the land in trust. I would love the park to be a living breathing national example of how a park should be run in an environmentally sustainable manner. It would be run with no chemical use, providing its own renewable energy and water and ensuring that new plantings are designed to encourage local wildlife, while still providing for all the other needs a park provides for the community such as sport and play.

Soon after being elected as a councillor, the council started redeveloping a large section of our local area with 5,000 new homes. I persuaded the council to carry out an environmental audit of the project by Brighton University. If we ensured they were insulated to Swedish standards, and had the latest in efficient boilers then they would have lower heating bills. If we ensured that only energy-saving bulbs and only energy-efficient washing machines and fridges were installed then they would have lower electricity bills. If we ensured that they had showers, spray taps and water barrels installed then they would have lower water bills, and if composting facilities were included the council would not have to waste money collecting such waste.

When the environmental audit of the redevelopment was published, it found that the new housing would not reach 'affordable warmth targets', ie people living on social incomes would not be able to afford to heat their new homes and many of the families moving into the new properties would suffer from water poverty. This in a country with thousands of litres of rain falling for free on each roof every year!

What was great about the audit process was how the project managers responded to it. After reading the audit, they became enthusiastic supporters of incorporating many of the recommendations. They significantly improved the energy-efficiency rating of the homes and started putting in showers and rain barrels as standard features, which meant that new tenants could reduce their water bills. They also installed composting units in the gardens, which reduced the council's waste-removal bills.

Over 4 million people in the UK suffer from fuel poverty – ie they spend more than 10 per cent of their income on heating, cooking and other energy use – contributes to over 35,000 extra deaths among the elderly every winter in England alone. The human and health-service costs of this fuel poverty are immense. Thankfully, the new homes built after the environmental audit now will not suffer from such fuel poverty and shows that environmental and social justice can go hand in hand.

Having seen the positive progress made in the housing project, I decided to apply the process to the other organisation that I was personally involved in as a trustee, Groundwork Southwark. This is a local environmental charity set up to improve the environment of the entire local inner-city area around where I live. My fellow trustees agreed with me that the charity should include an environmental audit with its annual accounts.

The process unleashed a whole raft of suggestions from staff, and we produced a paper detailing current good practice with suggestions for improvement. We also produced a new environmental checklist for our projects, which included the following questions:

1. Could the amount of waste produced by the project be reduced?

2. Could unavoidable waste materials from the project be recycled?

3. Could renewable energy sources be used for any energy requirements of the project?

4. Could water efficiency/rain-harvesting be included in the project?

5. Could any new materials required be sourced from recycled materials?

6. Could native plants that feed local wildlife be included?

7. Could energy-efficiency measures be included, eg could motion sensors be used to cut down on unnecessary light or energy use?

8. Could recycled paper and other materials be used in any promotions/publicity for the project?

9. Could provision for sustainable transport be included in the project, eg for cycling?

10. Could we use organic food and drinks for any launches or receptions associated with the project?

After only its first year, the environmental audit has already produced real change in how the charity approaches its projects, releasing a lot of creative goodwill from the staff.

But the icing on the cake was when my colleagues got our local authority to instigate environmental auditing in 2003–4. The audit has been carried out, the recommendations made and a programme of improvements agreed. The audit had immediately identified over £7,000 worth of immediate energy-management savings which more than covered the cost of the audit before any report had even been drafted.

While the audit identified some areas of good practice, it identified a large number of areas where the organisation could easily, without significant investment, substantially improve its environmental performance. My favourite example of a practice that could be reformed – which I think that anyone familiar with large organisations will identify with – was that in one of the main meeting rooms, despite it being unused at the time, the auditors found the lights were on was broad daylight, the windows were open, the heating was on maximum (despite it being a sunny day in late April) and the air-conditioning was on.

Among the list of recommendation from the audit that have been agreed to are:

- Appointing an 'environmental champion' in every workplace in the organisation.

- Immediate environmental good practice training for all facilities managers.

- Negotiating with cleaning/security companies to ensure that all equipment was turned off at night.

- Establishing cycle pools in all departments for staff use on business.

- Instigating a new green purchasing code.

- Ensuring that all new PCs have low-energy flat LCD screens.

- All paper products in future to be bought from recycled sources except where the product is not available.

- A programme of insulating all hot water and heating pipes and valves.

- Doubling the monthly staff cycle allowance.

- Immediate introduction of recycling schemes across all departments.

- Immediate programme of installing loft insulation, fixing broken heating controls.

- Better zoning of heating systems.

- Commissioning a report on feasibility of a major Combined Heat & Power (CHP) energy scheme across the organisation.

Many of these recommendations would apply to any large organisation with which you may be associated. Having read the report, I allowed myself an imaginary glass of champagne in celebration of seeing what I had first proposed in 1994 finally come to fruition!

Having been elected as a councillor, I started attending the party's annual national conference as a delegate and soon got involved in working to bring the environmental work I was doing at the local level up to a national level. My first initiative was a motion to conference calling on the federal party to use only 100 per cent recycled paper. I believe in politics by example and thought if the party intended having an annual environmental audit of the government when we got into power, then we needed to start practising now by doing it ourselves. While a seemingly small request, I found myself on a steep learning curve about how politics works at national level and how to stimulate and promote change in a large institution. The immediate response from the then party establishment was one of fear. They were frightened by how much it would cost and by how much it would require current practice to change. This is a fairly normal reaction to new proposals. It took three or four attempts before I persuaded the democratically elected conference committee to accept the proposal for debate and I was delighted when the conference passed the motion.

They still resisted switching to recycled paper on cost grounds, so I asked for permission to fundraise for the £1,000 annual cost. Just a week later at a work reception a man came up and asked if I was a Lib Dem, as he recognised my name from some articles I had written. I replied that I was and we got chatting and I mentioned my idea about the party being an example of how we would run the country sustainably. He asked me how much extra the recycled paper would cost and immediately offered to pay the entire cost by himself. Needless to say, not having tried any national fundraising before, I was gob-smacked to find I had it all raised without lifting a finger. Therefore that year, 1996, the party's headquarters switched its annual 2 million sheets of paper consumption to recycled paper and has continued to do so ever since.

The next stage in my environmental activism at the national level resulted from a simple letter that I received from Survival International, an international body working with indigenous peoples across the globe, to protect their interests and promote their human rights. I joined them after I came back from the Amazon, as a small gesture of support for the Yanomami. One of the key campaign tools they use is to ask members to write to various government officials in the country where indigenous people are under threat. The letter I received was a request to write to President Suharto of Indonesia about the plight of the Amungme tribe whose land was being mined by a subsidiary of Rio Tinto Zinc. The mining corporation was intending to slice the top off a mountain in its search for mineral ores. The Amungme's spiritual beliefs involved one's soul migrating to the peak of this mountain when one died. They also claimed that there was significant danger of poisons leaking into the local water sources.

I was about to write the requested letter when a small bell went off in the back of my mind. Had I not read that the party's then leader, Paddy Ashdown, had appointed a director of Rio

Tinto Zinc to be the director of our campaign for the 1997 general election? I checked and found that I was right – it was Lord Richard Holme, then an executive director for external affairs for RTZ. I knew that if I wrote to Suharto instead of Ashdown, I would be acting hypocritically. I therefore wrote to Paddy Ashdown expressing my concern about the dual role held by Lord Holme. He wrote back stating that he had been assured by Lord Holme that RTZ's record was exemplary and that he accepted Richard's assurances.

Well, I am not one to be put off by a piece of corporate spin, so I started researching RTZ. It had been condemned by the United Nations for its activities in South Africa during the apartheid regime. It was the world's largest private producer of uranium and it was the target of numerous campaigns by environmental groups for various alleged misdeeds across the planet. It even had an environmental pressure group devoted solely to exposing its human rights and environmental record, called PaRTiZans. I assembled a large information pack from all the NGOs (non-governmental organisations) that were campaigning against RTZ's activities and sent it to all the members of the party's Federal Executive (FE) which acts as the national board of the party.

I argued, how could one person promote RTZ with its human rights and environmental record and its status as the largest private uranium producer in the world and simultaneously be in charge of a general election campaign for a party for whom human rights, respect for the environment and opposition to nuclear power was at the heart of their campaign? It was frankly untenable.

The FE having never even heard of me, an unknown local councillor from Southwark, responded not by asking Lord Holme to choose between the two roles but rather asked officers to draw up 'a media strategy' should the issue blow up. I was disappointed when I heard but did not give up. Simon

Hughes, one of the party's members of parliament, was deputed by the leader to try and sort the problem. He organised a meeting at parliament with Lord Holme to thrash the issue out. The meeting was gruelling. I had never met Lord Holme before and the meeting was attended by a phalanx of the party's national employees. I was extremely nervous as I felt I was well and truly in at the deep end. I presented my case and Lord Holme responded. It went on for almost two hours but Simon's efforts at mediation failed.

On my way home from the next national party conference, I read an article in the Evening Standard (London's only evening newspaper) in which Lord Holme claimed the conference had endorsed him. Incensed, I resolved there and then to stand for election to the party's Federal Executive on an anti-RTZ ticket. Despite having almost zero national profile and the party taking legal advice to edit my election address, I was elected. I had now gone from being a dancer to a member of the board of one of Britain's three major political parties in just four years. It is astonishing what being an environmental activist will sometimes accidentally lead to! And so a few weeks later, terrified, I faced my first Federal Executive meeting at the party's national headquarters, with a motion on the agenda from me demanding that Lord Richard Holme choose between the two roles.

I entered the boardroom that evening, and felt a little daunted as I surveyed all the most senior people in the party ranged round the meeting table – the leader, the chief whip, members of the Lords, members of parliament, senior councillors, elected representatives from across Britain and of course Lord Holme. I hadn't met many of them before. When it came to my motion, the leader announced that if the FE agreed to my request, he would resign immediately. Not exactly how I envisaged my first meeting at national level! In the end only one member of the executive supported me and that was

Lembit Opik, who was a local councillor in Newcastle at the time but who was later to become MP for Montgomeryshire and Leader of the Welsh Liberal Democrats.

However, while I failed with my objective, the FE agreed that in future such appointments should not be in the gift of the leader but should be democratically chosen by the Federal Executive. Lord Holme has thankfully since then retired from RTZ and no senior Liberal Democrat has taken his place on the RTZ board, as had been the custom up until then.

I have been elected to the Federal Executive almost every year since then, successfully applying to be a member of many national policy commissions, seeking always to ensure that we moved in a progressive direction on environmental issues. I was also busy serving on the Genetic Engineering, Globalisation, Defence and Rural Affairs (despite coming from inner-city London) national Policy Working Groups. I succeeded in helping to get policies in favour of compulsory labelling of GM foods, the banning of GM for farm animals, and for the necessity of international environmental treaties to take precedence over WTO rules, a renewable energy economy and a national pesticide-reduction strategy, through the various committees and then through party conference when the papers were finally debated there. It just shows what an ordinary environmentalist can achieve when thrown in the deep end politically. You really can swim.

I was also pleased to get recognition of the fact that we need to tackle the emerging scarcity of natural resources such as oil and water if we are to avoid future global conflicts over them. We achieved agreement that we should oppose all arms sales to non-democratic countries and to countries that abuse human rights. I was delighted at how I was able to help advance environmental issues in these committees, even though I was basically an amateur activist. As each issue arose I made time to go and be briefed by the relevant NGOs and I also found that many of the so-called experts were not very good at political argument. I was able to not only survive but help win a number of battles that environmentalists in the party were delighted with. Just because someone is armed with a title such as professor, director of some international institute or even rear admiral does not mean that you can't debate constructively with them, provided you've done your research beforehand, spoken to other experts in the field and stick to your basic principles.

A couple of years after I was first elected to the FE, I resigned from my post as manager of the Islington Chamber of Commerce in order to work full time on the campaign to stop our party leader Paddy Ashdown from making a secret deal with the British Prime Minister Tony Blair that would have destroyed the party's independence. I had set up a group a year previously within the party called 'New Radicalism', whose purpose was not only to campaign for a continuing independent, mainstream, green-liberal voice in British politics, but which also develop a policy and philosophical basis for such independence. One of the founding five basic tenets of 'New Radicalism' was that clean air, clean water, clean soil and clean non-GM-contaminated food are ours by right and the coming generations' by right. I knew environmentalism was not a central concern of Blairism, the neo-conservative political philosophy associated with the British Prime Minister, and was very worried that we would lose our ability to criticise the government constructively if Blair managed to neutralise us.

The putative deal was never endorsed and died on the vine over time. Paddy Ashdown resigned as leader not long after. Thus, we were able to ensure that there was an independent pro-environment voice preserved in Parliament which continued to keep up the pressure for a radical change in government action on environmental issues.

I was then privileged to be elected Deputy Chair of the party's Federal Executive in 2002 and was then re-elected in 2003, which allowed me to pursue my campaign to make the party a living, breathing example of environmental sustainability. One of the highlights of my term was when I was the Liberal Democrat speaker at the largest wartime peace rally ever held in Britain after the US/UK 2003 Iraqi invasion. I had often urged our new party leader Charles Kennedy to take a lead on identifying our dependence on Middle Eastern and Asian oil as being one of the great threats to world peace, as well as contributing to the potential global catastrophe of global warming. That morning I realised I had a unique opportunity to deliver that message myself.

I suddenly felt frightened at being thought completely eccentric at speaking to such a huge audience and telling them that, as they themselves used electricity and drove cars, they were therefore part of the oil economy and they too held some of the blame for these oil wars. I wanted to tell them to go home and stop using their cars so much and to get on the web and switch to a renewable-energy supplier for their homes. I did, however, find the courage to tell the huge crowd of over half a million people to do so, and to my delight they didn't laugh, but heard me and cheered in agreement instead.

I came off the platform afterwards shaking but really moved that I had managed to say my truth. It takes a lot less courage for me to repeat the same message here in this book, but I hope that you too will hear and not only agree but actually start to make the changes you need to in your own home, work and life in the wider world. It still astonishes me how my journey and commitment to the environment since my visit to the Yanomami just over ten years ago led me to a high office in a major political party, and to having the incredible privilege to speak to such a huge crowd of people at such a special event.

This book has opened up a new avenue for me to spread the message that our environment needs urgent care and attention. Millions of people of our children's generation should not be in danger of having their homes and their land flooded or be in fear of starvation due to climate disasters because we did not take action soon enough. I have no idea where your new environmental lifestyle is now going to take you, but I wish you lots of success wherever your commitment to our planet takes you next. I hope it brings you at least some of the fun and excitement I am having along the way. Good luck!

Resources

Chapter 2 Waste Not, Want Not

Replaceable-head toothbrushes are available worldwide from www.naturalcollection.com.

Information on nappies in the UK can be found on www.realnappy.com.

In the US, for natural diapers see www.ecowise.com.

For information on women's menstrual products, cosmetics etc see www.wen.org.uk.

To source recycled products in the UK see www.recycledproducts.org.

For a database on where to recycle different materials in the UK by postcode see www.recycle-more.co.uk.

To eliminate unwanted faxes and mail in the UK try www.fpsonline.org.uk and in the US it's www.dmaconsumers.org.

Chapter 3 The Water of Life

Information on rain-harvesters in the UK is available from www.rainharvesting.co.uk or in London from www.constructionresources.com. The Environment Agency also has an information leaflet available from paula.wood@environment-agency.gov.uk.

In the US, the Texas Water Development Board provides a free online guide to rain-harvesting at www.twdb.state.tx.us.

The Green Pages website provides a list of grey-water recycling companies worldwide at www.eco-web.com.

Information on drought-resistant plants and gardening can be found in the monthly free online magazine published by High Country Gardens at www.highcountrygardens.com.

The National Childbirth Trust (UK) runs a large series of sales of really good value reused children's toys, clothes, cots, go-karts etc, and they maintain a directory of these with dates and locations on their website at www.nctpregnancyandbabycare.com.

Chapter 4 Positively Fuelling our Lives

A list of solar water heating supply businesses in the US can be found at www.energy.sourceguides.com. In the UK, www.greenenergy.org.uk provides information and a list of suppliers

Climate Care provides a CO_2 calculator for various individual actions such as air travel at www.co2.org, while a personal lifestyle CO_2 calculator can be found at www.iclei.org/co2/co2calc.htm.

To change your domestic electricity supplier to a 100-per-cent renewable supplier in the UK, go to the Good Energy website at www.unit-e.co.uk. They were judged to be the best supplier in 2002 by Friends of the Earth UK. To change in the US try www.sterlingplanet.com.

For information on solar electricity in the US try the Solar Electric Power Association at www.solarelectricpower.org.

For a list of worldwide suppliers of domestic windmills, micro-hydro systems and photovoltaics (solar electric systems) go to the Green Pages at www.eco-web.com.

For information on grants for renewable energy systems for domestic homes in the UK go to the Energy Savings Trust website at www.est.org.uk.

Chapter 5 Gardening – Our Direct Link With Nature

Lists of native plants by postcode in the UK can be found at the Natural History Museum website at www.nhm.ac.uk, while in the US the Lady Bird Johnson Wildflower Centre provides lists of native plants by state at www.wildflower.org.

Bat boxes can be got in the US at www.batcon.org or in the UK from the Royal Society for the Protection of Birds (RSPB) at www.rspb.org.uk who also sell bird boxes.

Information on organic gardening/agriculture can be found in the UK from the Soil Association at www.soilassociation.org or from the Henry Doubleday Research Association at www.hdra.org.uk. The HDRA provides information on organic farming and agriculture for developing countries too. In the US, information on organics may be found at the National Organic Program website at www.ams.usda.gov/nop.

Information on how to garden according to the principles of Permaculture can be found at www.permaculture.net.

Information on the world's rainforests can be found at www.rainforestweb.org.

A wide-ranging database of pesticides and their toxicity is maintained by the Pesticides Action Network at www.pesticideinfo.org.

Chapter 6 Real Food or Chemical Food?

Information on vegetarianism can be found in the UK from The Vegetarian Society at www.vegsoc.org and in North America from the North American Vegetarian Society at www.navs-online.org.

Information on breastfeeding can be found in the UK from The Breastfeeding Network at www.breastfeedingnetwork.org.uk, while is the US it can be found at the United States Breastfeeding Committee's website at www.breastfeeding.org.

A directory of organic food services such as restaurants, accommodation, shops, farm-shops and organic-box schemes can be found in the UK at the Soil Association website at www.soilassociation.org.

The Organic Trading Association maintains a world directory of organic food businesses at its website on www.ota.com.

Chapter 7 Home & Personal Maintenance

A directory of UK suppliers of reclaimed timber can be found at www.recycle.mcmail.com.

Natural cosmetics and sunscreens can be found at www.tlcinabottle.co.uk.

The US website www.sustainableabc.com has a directory of green architects, designers, interior decorators, landscape architects, builders etc. While in the UK the Friends of the Earth website has a very wide range of green links, which includes a directory of green building services websites at www.foe.co.uk.

Advice on energy saving and government grants for domestic houses and businesses in the UK can be found at the Energy Savings Trust website www.est.org.uk. In the US energy efficiency information listed state by state can be found at the website www.eia.doe.gov/emeu/efficiency/energy.

The website for listings of green community currencies in the UK is found at www.letslink.org.uk.

The web address for natural hemp products is www.thehempshop.net.

The international web listings for each country with a Forest Stewardship Council (FSC) initiative on certified, sustainable timber products are found under the documents section at www.fscoax.org. This includes a large range of countries across the world, including the US and UK.

Listings of businesses involved in green building supplies across the US are found at www.ecobusinesslinks.com.

Chapter 8 Saving the Planet at Work

There is a comprehensive list of Europe-wide green electricity tariffs both for businesses and domestic homes at www.greenprices.com.

Small businesses in the UK can get information about a free waste audit of their companies from the government agency Envirowise at www.envirowise.gov.uk. They also have a free helpline for environmental queries from small businesses at 0800 585794.

Environmentally sustainable office products can be found at the online Green Stationery Shop in the UK at www.greenstat.co.uk.

Comprehensive information on water conservation and services can be found in the US at www.awwa.org and businesses in the UK can get information from the Environment Agency at www.environment-agency.gov.uk/subjects/waterres.

The environmentally-friendly automobile breakdown rescue association in the United States is the Better World Club, which can be found at www.betterworldclub.com while in the UK it is the Environmental Transport Association at www.eta.co.uk.

Fair trade product and supplier information can be found at www.fairtrade.org.uk.

A worldwide directory of over 6,000 environmental businesses and suppliers, listed by category and from over 140 countries can be found at www.eco-web.com. The list covers everything from renewable energy to soil management and recycling businesses.

Over 2,000 environmental products and services for business can be found in the US at www.greenpages.org, where they are listed by state and by category.

Chapter 9 Out and About

A worldwide directory of car-sharing initiatives can be found at www.eartheasy.com/live_car_sharing, this covers many European countries including the UK and also covers North America, including Canada.

A US directory of car-sharing initiatives can be found at www.carsharing.net.

A small but growing listing of green holidays from around the world can be found at www.ecocities.net/holidays or at the UK site at www.green.solutions.com.

Information on ethical investments can be found in the UK at the website www.uksif.org or in the US at www.ecobusinesslinks.com/links/investments.

International environmental membership campaigning organisations include:

Friends of the Earth International at www.foei.org. This has a list of national Friends of the Earth organisations across the globe.

Greenpeace International can be found at www.greenpeace.org/international_en.

The organisation working for indigenous people's rights across the globe is Survival International and they can be found at www.survival-international.org.

The World Wide Fund for Nature (WWF) has its website at www.panda.org (this really is their address!).

And finally, as someone who has embraced political activity as one means to create a better future for our planet, can I suggest that you join a political party of your choice and campaign within them for a higher priority for the environment. Just look up their website in whatever country you live in and you should be able to join online.

The following are a few political web addresses in the UK and US: Green Liberal Democrats www.greenlibdems.org.uk, The Green Party www.greenparty.org.uk, The Labour Party www.labour.org.uk, The Conservative Party www.conservatives.com, The Republican Party www.rnc.org, The Democrat Party www.democrats.org, The Green Party (US) www.gp.org.

Acknowledgements

There I was on the barriers outside the American Embassy in London, organising yet another candle-lit peace vigil during the run up to the invasion of Iraqi in Spring 2003, when a woman came up to me and introduced herself as Sheena Dewan. She proceeded to tell me, there and then, that she wanted me to write a book for her publishing house. The book she wanted was for people who, having sorted out their recycling, wanted to know what else they could do to help save our precious planet. She had noticed that an environmentally-friendly lifestyle can save you money and thought this needed to be brought to people's attention.

I was thrilled and flattered to be asked to do it, and hope that the finished product that now lies in your hands will help inspire you to fulfil that original vision. We are lucky to have such an independent liberal publishing house. So naturally my first thanks goes to Sheena for trusting me to deliver for them. Second, but only by a smidgen, are the thanks due to Charlotte Cole, my editor, whose hard work, advice and willingness to challenge me have ensured that my initial rough manuscript was transformed into the book that we both wanted.

Thanks are also due most importantly to my boss Jack Haslam, whose support and patience ensured the working hours flexibility that allowed me the space and freedom to create and complete this book. My gratitude must also extend to a whole host of others. These include all my other work

235

colleagues at The Lord's Taverners for their patience during this time; to all my colleagues at the Groundwork Trust and the Liberal Democrats for allowing me to experiment with environmental auditing on them; to Martin Cotterell for being an inspiring renewable energy pioneer; to Chris Dunham, my Palestinian peace and solar electricity monitor(!); to my Yanomami hosts, with whom my too short sojourn taught me that it is possible to have a civilisation that does not destroy our planet and who opened my shuttered eyes to the destruction that was being manifested all around me in my Western culture; to Danielle Byrne for guiding me in my initial environmental activism; to Norman Baker MP for allowing me to use his research on the lack of UK recycling; to my fellow musketeers Kirsten and Mary; and last but by no means least to my dear friend Pauline Davis, whose spiritual and loving support through this whole project was more valuable than I can ever hope to repay.

With love to you all,
Donnachadh
Peckham, London

About the Author

Born in County Tipperary in the Republic of Ireland, Donnachadh McCarthy spent four years studying medicine at the National University of Ireland before leaving to train as a ballet dancer. He moved to London in 1986 and achieved his dream of dancing with the Royal Opera Ballet. An invitation to join an expedition to visit the Yanomami people in the heart of the Amazonian rainforest radically transformed his life. Realising how our consumer lifestyle was destroying the rainforest and these people, he resolved to halt this process on his return. He first tackled his own life: Donnachadh's home was the first in London to sell solar electricity to the national grid. It also has a rain-harvester, which provides nearly all his water. Active campaigning on environmental issues gave rise to Donnachadh's election to his local council where he led the improvement to the council's environmental performance, for which it won national awards. Subsequently, he was elected as Deputy Chair of Britain's third biggest political party, where he increased the emphasis on environmental issues such as global warming and genetic modification. He continues his campaigning to transform individual and the wider country's environmental performance.

Ethical Shopping
Where to Shop, What to Buy and What to Do to
Make a Difference

William Young and Richard Welford

How ethical are Sainsbury's, Nokia, Gap, Nike and The Body
Shop? This handbook lists hundreds of companies and details
whether they have developed socially responsible codes of
conduct for their suppliers.

As concern grows about the conditions of workers in developing countries, this book contains everything you need to
know about ethical and fair trade. Covering a wide range of
goods and services, including clothes, DIY, electronics, food,
furniture and beauty, *Ethical Shopping* provides everything you
need to shop with a clear conscience.

This is a practical guide to making ethical shopping decisions.
It puts the essential information in the wider context of
globalisation and consumer power.

ISBN: 1-904132-08-1
UK: £7.99
www.fusionpress.co.uk

Sold Out
The True Cost of Supermarket Shopping

William Young

'The supermarkets have pretty much got an armlock on you people at the moment.'
Tony Blair to farmers at Hartpury Agricultural College

Supermarkets have become dominant players in the globalised marketplace and as a result have revolutionised British shopping habits. The 'Big Four' bring the world's food (and increasingly most other high street products and services) to large, bright and clean one-stop stores at affordable prices.

But while they satisfy every 'need' and 'want' of consumers, there are other impacts on society and the environment. For the first time in one book, William Young explores the wider cost of customer satisfaction to the local community, other retailers, the environment and farmers in the UK and worldwide. Thoroughly researched, this is a timely and sometimes disturbing investigation that explores whether supermarkets are a force for good in the UK.

ISBN: 1-904132-40-5
UK: £10.99
www.visionpaperbacks.co.uk

Seal Wars
My 25-Year Struggle to Save the Seals

Paul Watson

As a young boy, Paul Watson asked his uncle to take him to the beach to see the seals. Arriving, he found trails of blood along the ice floes to the shoreline and the seals' skinless bodies. It was a scene that would haunt him for years.

Seal Wars is the story of one man's extraordinary efforts to end the slaughter of the harp seal. Driven by his childhood experience, Watson has taken on brutal sealers, obfuscating governments and even the environmental movement he co-founded. From acting as a human shield to blocking harbours and sinking boats, this self-styled buccaneer has never given up trying to ban an unprofitable and bloody 'industry'.

In Seal Wars, Watson reveals the history of the seal hunt and tells the powerful and extraordinary tale of his commitment to protecting the seals no matter what the personal cost.

ISBN: 1-904132-37-5
UK: £10.99
www.visionpaperbacks.co.uk